LONDON
A to Z

By John Metcalf

Decorated by Edward Bawden

With a new introduction by Peyton Skipwith

D1353784

Thames & Hudson

First published in the UK in 1953 by Andre Deutsch Limited

This new paperback edition first published in 2016 by Thames & Hudson Ltd, London

British Library Cataloguing-in-Publication Data
A catalogue record for this book is available from the British Library

ISBN 978-0-500-29247-1

Printed and bound in China by Everbest Printing Co. Ltd

To find out about all our publications, please visit **www.thamesandhudson.com**. There you can subscribe to our e-newsletter, browse or download our current catalogue, and buy any titles that are in print.

INTRODUCTION

The concept behind John Metcalf's *London A to Z* is brilliant – and yet so simple. I don't know how it came about. Perhaps one summer's day in 1952, sitting in a country garden and chatting with friends in dappled sunlight, a glass of wine to hand, someone said: 'thousands of people are going to descend on London next June for the coronation, and what they will require is a pocket-size guidebook that they can consult for their day-to-day requirements – theatres, hospitals, pubs, how to get around...'. However it arose, the idea caught on, and the British publisher André Deutsch got together with John Metcalf – if there really was such a person – to do just that. They clearly didn't want a dry-as-dust lexicon; rather, something that would give the bemused visitor an insight not only into London, but into Londoners as well.

In those now distant days there were still plenty of true Londoners – Cockneys, that is – around, though even then Metcalf described them as a dying breed. He and Deutsch clearly thought that London could not be comprehended without an appreciation of Cockney humour, which was also threatened with extinction, along with rhyming slang, its tribal language. Metcalf may have been comforted that the latter would survive and continue to develop by the fact that 'the old phrase for gin, "a barrel and pin", ha[d] been ousted in recent years in favour of "a Vera Lynn".' Alas, I fear his optimism was misplaced. Cockney is now a subject reserved exclusively for sentimentalists and linguistic scholars.

There were two editions of *London A to Z,* a hardback and a paperback, retailing for five shillings and half a crown (25p and 12½p) respectively. The blurb on the dust jacket of the hardback edition described it as 'the guide-book for: Accuracy, Brevity, Convenience, Detail,

Easy reading, Facts, Gourmets, Humour, Information, Junketing, Knowledge, Liveliness, Method, Night life, Originality, Parties, Quick-reference, Reliability, Sight-seeing, Time-saving, Usefulness, Visitors, Xmas, Yourself, Zest', thus giving the potential purchaser a tantalising taste of the guide's uses and humour.

The text under 'A' kicks off with ACHILLES' STATUE in Hyde Park – 'one of the bigger, bronzier, nuder of Victorian statues, it was, remarkably enough, erected by the women of England to honour the memory of (if not to resemble) the Duke of Wellington' – continuing via DICKENS' LONDON and TURKISH BATHS to 'Z' for ZEBRA CROSSINGS and ZOOS. The crossings, described as 'relative newcomers to London', came with a caveat from the author: 'The theory is that once you've actually managed to establish one foot on one stripe, all the traffic stops and allows you to walk across unharmed. This, as I say, is the theory. Don't put too much faith in it, or you're liable to leave London with less feet than you started out with.'

Metcalf could, and did, inject a dry humour into both the selection of his headline topics – from ACHILLES to ZEBRA CROSSINGS, the sublime to the quotidian – and the entries themselves, but some form of decoration was needed to complete the package. And who better to supply it than Edward Bawden? By then Bawden had already illustrated D. M. Low's *London is London* and John Betjeman's essay on 'London Railway Stations', included in Max Parrish's anthology *Flower of Cities: A Book of London,* as well as having drawn delightfully quirky posters for two of Ealing Studios' best-loved comedies, *Hue and Cry* and *The Titfield Thunderbolt.* He had also just produced a *City of London* poster (1952) for London Transport, for which he had assembled a variety of images into a collage. In a letter to Harold Hutchinson, London Transport's publicity officer at the time, he wrote, 'I have shown bits & pieces of the following:- St Paul's, the Monument, Bow Church, the Guildhall, Leadenhall Market & the Old Bailey.' It was a formula he would repeat in simplified form for the appealing cover of both editions of *London A to Z*.

The hunch that thousands of people would come to London proved correct. They converged from all corners of the British Isles, but also from the Dominions, from America and from the few remaining remnants of Britain's fast-declining Empire – and they bought copies. Travellers from further afield apparently favoured the hardback (or perhaps only that edition was available to them), as you are more likely to find it in second-hand and antiquarian bookshops in Brisbane or Montreal than in Birmingham or Manchester.

Apart from the new queen, Elizabeth II, the star of the coronation procession was the monumentally over-sized Queen Salote of Tonga, who, despite the rain, insisted on riding in an open carriage. She was accompanied by a small man, popularly and humorously described as 'her lunch'. As a fourteen-year-old schoolboy on one of my earliest visits to London, I had the good fortune to view her and the rest of the procession from a balcony in Park Lane. Royalty aside, the one feature indelibly engraved on the memories of all those who were there that day, whether as honoured guests or spectators, is the rain. That first week of June 1953 was the wettest week of the wettest summer England had witnessed for a long time, rendering Metcalf's section on the UMBRELLA particularly pertinent. 'There are two kinds of umbrella' he says, 'those that are used, and those that are carried.' The former could be seen in great numbers on suburban trains and in the City, 'flapping and rusty and everyday looking', while the latter, which he describes as the twentieth century's equivalent of the sword, 'are never under any circumstance opened', but could be seen parading along Bond Street, Piccadilly and St James's. For the purchase of either sort the reader was referred to 'Umbrellas, Shooting-sticks, Walking-sticks', a subsection of SHOPPING, with the direction: 'For smart ones: Swaine, Adeney, Briggs, 185 Piccadilly. For not-so-smart: any Lost Property Sales Office.' If the bemused visitor then turned to the paragraph headed LOST PROPERTY OFFICES he – for surely it would have been a he – would have found the useful advice that should you wish to 'buy an umbrella, a raincoat or a suitcase cheap, these sort of things, lonely and unclaimed, are on sale at Lost Property Sales Offices,' followed by half a dozen addresses.

The endearing quirkiness of this little volume is enhanced by the kaleidoscopic randomness of the alphabetical approach as well as by Metcalf's humour. Immediately following the paragraph on Lost Property Offices is one headed 'LOVELY SWEET VIOLETS' and accompanied by one of Bawden's distinctive line drawings, a bright little woman looking a bit like Worzel Gummidge's Aunt Sally, who is seated before a basket of violets. The text informs the reader that 'lovely sweet violets' was one of the last remaining street cries among 'the septuagenarian flower girls of Piccadilly Circus' – Cockneys to their very toenails – and that you could, in 1953 at least, still occasionally hear the cry 'in the purlieus of Haymarket and Coventry Street.' Metcalf notes that 'the violets are dearer now; but they are still as sweet.' Even when it was first published, *London A to Z* was tinged with such touches of nostalgia; reading it now, as someone who has lived in London for more than half a century, the nostalgia is greatly increased. Turning from 'LOVELY SWEET VIOLETS' to FLOWER SHOPS, the names Constance Spry and Moyses Stevens spring out from the short list of the author's favourites. Both are now gone, as are most of the restaurants, although a few old names survive under different management. The same applies

vi

to virtually all the art dealers, though I am happy to say The Fine Art Society, my own old firm, is still in the same location and has the same telephone number, even if you would need one of those old telephones with a rotary dial to decode and ring 'MAY' for Mayfair.

London A to Z was generous in providing the addresses of most of the institutions and shops it featured, as well as the telephone numbers with their now long-vanished exchanges – REG, TEM, WHI, GER, AMB, PAD, etc. Whoever devised that London dialling system was a potential code-breaker for Bletchley Park; some of the local exchanges – MAYfair, REGent, WHItehall – were based on well-known streets or districts, while others, such as AMBassador, were obscure. It was sometimes possible to make words out of the seven-digit combination. My favourite was that of a catering firm we patronised at The Fine Art Society while we were setting up an exhibition of nineteenth-century sculpture and working regularly until midnight. We just had to dial CHICKEN (CHIswick 2536) with our order and the meals would duly arrive. I was reminded of this on seeing that Moyses Stevens offered an all-night flower-delivery service. What a romantic idea that at any hour of the night, on impulse, you could have flowers delivered to your love of the moment.

Metcalf's counterpoint to such innocent romance is under 'V' for VICE. He reasonably claimed that London was remarkably free from 'organised vice, largely due to the stolid incorruptibility of an underpaid police force,' but did advise the unsuspecting visitor not to believe 'everything you hear, and in particular don't believe the spiv who hints at splendid goings-on in a little club he knows in Soho: you'll probably end up drinking filthy cocktails with a rabbit-faced blonde called Rosie, while six large men get larger and larger, and the room smaller.' No late-night roses for Rosie here!

The sixty years or so separating the original publication of *London A to Z* and this reissue have witnessed the decimation, even annihilation, of certain subjects about which Metcalf expatiated, such as SECRETARIAL SERVICES and the tracks listed under GREYHOUND RACING, while other categories, notably HOTELS and THEATRES, have proved more enduring. In the HOTELS section most of the big names survive, though some, such as the Berkeley, are no longer in the same location. Here, once again, Metcalf made fine distinctions, citing Claridges, the Connaught, the Ritz and Brown's as 'perhaps the most exclusive', thus neatly separating them from the Savoy and the Dorchester, which he described as 'the minkiest'. The minks may be fewer today, but otherwise his judgment remains intact. More surprising is the demise – or perhaps the erstwhile existence – of such museums as the Royal United Services Museum in Whitehall and the Home Office Industrial Museum, which apparently specialised in 'safety appliances'.

Edward Bawden's keen eye, versatility and delight in individuality made him the ideal illustrator for *London A to Z*. He employed both pen and ink as well as linocut, a medium in which he was a master. I have known sculptors who talked of 'drawing in clay', and in much the same manner Bawden could 'doodle in lino'. He clearly used lino blocks for the cover and frontispiece, but also, I am sure, for some of the little vignettes, such as that of the double-decker bus with the 'clippie' (conductress) swinging blithely from the deck and the newsvendor under FLEET STREET.

Simultaneously with *London A to Z*, Bawden was producing bright and lively publicity material for Fortnum & Mason, one of the still extant stores listed under 'Women's Shopping' in SHOPPING, where you could get 'everything from a pin to a *peignoir*'. It would probably be deemed sexist today to have such a category as 'Women's

Shopping', and in our age of speedy obsolescence the section below it headed 'Stocking Repairs' would certainly be redundant. However, the names of some of those long-lost West End stores, such as Bourne & Hollingsworth, Marshall & Snelgrove, Swears & Wells and Robinson & Cleaver, still resonate: they are the stuff of poetry, straight from the pen of John Betjeman.

Nearly two-thirds of a century after its conception, this small book – random, idiosyncratic, poetic, whimsical and kaleidoscopic – has, like the London taxis Metcalf described on page 125, 'stood the test of years'. Future social historians would be well advised to turn to it for information, rather than to official Blue Books or other sources of statistics, as it so vividly conveys the life and spirit of mid-twentieth-century London. Today much of the metropolis as it existed then has succumbed to the inevitable advance of globalisation. Brick, the traditional London stock, is being replaced by glass and concrete, while the skyline, familiar since the days of Canaletto, has become virtually unrecognisable. But London – that 'flower of cities' – is still London, and in certain corners its Cockney spirit, as captured by John Metcalf in this book, lives on.

Peyton Skipwith, October 2015

LONDON A TO Z

LONDON A to Z

by
John Metcalf

Decorated by Edward Bawden

ANDRE DEUTSCH

ACKNOWLEDGEMENTS

I should like to express my thanks to the British Travel and Holidays Association, to the London County Council and to London Transport for the help and information that they have given me. J. M.

The references in square brackets that appear immediately after certain entries refer to the position of the places named on the map on pages 16 and 17.

A

ACHILLES' STATUE [C5] Hyde Park (near Hyde Park Corner). One of the bigger, bronzier, nuder of Victorian statues, it was, remarkably enough, erected by the women of England to honour the memory of (if not to resemble) the Duke of Wellington.

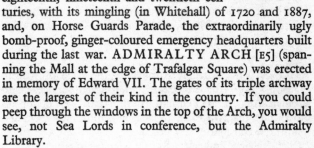

ADMIRALTY [E5] Whitehall (near Trafalgar Square). The headquarters of the most British Service brings together the eighteenth, nineteenth and twentieth centuries, with its mingling (in Whitehall) of 1720 and 1887, and, on Horse Guards Parade, the extraordinarily ugly bomb-proof, ginger-coloured emergency headquarters built during the last war. ADMIRALTY ARCH [E5] (spanning the Mall at the edge of Trafalgar Square) was erected in memory of Edward VII. The gates of its triple archway are the largest of their kind in the country. If you could peep through the windows in the top of the Arch, you would see, not Sea Lords in conference, but the Admiralty Library.

AIRLINES. All the big world airlines have London offices. The two British corporations—B.E.A., serving Europe and running inland services, and B.O.A.C., serving the rest of the world—will advise on everything from flying to Glasgow to chartering a 'plane to Peking. (See also TRAVEL AGENTS.)

Aer Lingus (Irish Air Lines), 19 Regent St. WHI 1080 SW1

Air Ceylon, 5 Regent St. W1   WHI 0411

Air France, 52 Haymarket, SW1	WHI 0971
Air India, 56 Haymarket, SW1	WHI 8506
Alitalia, Dorland Hall, Regent St. SW1	WHI 3285
Argentine Airlines, 42 Brook St. W1	REG 6941
Australian National Airways, 5 Regent St. SW1	WHI 0411
British European Airways, 14 Regent St. SW1	GER 9833
British Overseas Airways, 75 Regent St. SW1	REG 8444
El Al Israel Nat. Airlines, 295 Regent St. W1	LAN 8484
K.L.M., 196 Sloane St. SW1	SLO 9656
Pan American Airways, 193 Piccadilly, W1	REG 7292
Sabena, 205 Regent St. W1	MAY 8292
Scandinavian Airlines, 185 Regent St. W1	REG 6777
Spanish Airlines, 14 Regent St. SW1	WHI 3281
Swissair, 18 Regent St. SW1	GER 9833
Trans Canada Airlines, 27 Pall Mall, SW1	WHI 0851
Trans World Airlines, 200 Piccadilly, W1	REG 3211

AIRPORTS. Northolt Airport on the edge of Ruislip (Ruislip 3355)—for European and internal services—and London Airport at Feltham nearby (HOU 7711) for all others, are the two main passenger aerodromes. Others, mainly used on charter services, are:

Blackbushe, Camberley, Surrey (Camberly 1600)
Bovingdon, Hemel Hempstead, Herts (Bovingdon 2296)
Croydon, Surrey (CRO 7744)
Gatwick, Surrey (Crawley 680)
Lympne, Hythe, Kent (Hythe 6142)

AIR TERMINALS. The rule for these is: for Europe and for internal services you leave from Waterloo Air Terminal on the South Bank. This modern building was opened in May, 1953, and replaces the old Kensington Air Station in

Kensington High Street. For any of the other services, from Airways Terminal, Buckingham Palace Road, SW1 (VIC 2323); with the exception of K.L.M.—the Dutch airline —which uses its own air terminal at 196 Sloane Street, SW1 (SLO 9656). You can leave messages at the terminals or at the airports for arriving or departing friends.

ALBERT HALL [A5]—properly called the Royal Albert Hall—Kensington Gore, SW7 (KEN 8212). This great cake-tin of a place, which can hold over ten thousand people, was built in 1871 and is constantly in use for concerts, exhibitions, balls, recitals, boxing matches. Since the destruction of Queen's Hall during the war,  it is the headquarters of the famous Promenade Concerts (the Proms). It gets a thorough going-over every New Year's Eve when the Chelsea Arts Ball breaks out. The ALBERT MEMORIAL [A5] (opposite the Albert Hall) is a memorial, of course, to Queen Victoria's Prince Albert, and cost one hundred and twenty thousand good nineteenth-century pounds when it was completed in 1876. The Prince sits thirteen feet high in the middle. Long the target, through the twenties and thirties, of the mockery of aesthetes, it is now enjoying a certain vogue among the sort of people who use the words 'quaint' and 'charming'.

ALEXANDRA PALACE (Wood Green) sprawls heavily on the top of Muswell Hill. The television mast that tops it reminds you that it's the original home of B.B.C. Television and still (together with the Lime Grove Studios) the originating point of much that is seen on English screens. Its little racecourse holds attractive summer meetings where Gordon Richards seems to win nearly all the races.

ANNUAL EVENTS. Here are just a few recurring London events:

JANUARY

Circuses at Olympia, Harringay and Earl's Court.
London Fashion Openings (last week of the month).
Pantomimes at many theatres.

Schoolboys' Own Exhibition at Royal Horticultural Hall, Westminster.

FEBRUARY

Cruft's Dog Show at Olympia (beginning of the month).

MARCH

Ideal Home Exhibition at Olympia.
Oxford and Cambridge Boat Race, Putney to Mortlake (end of the month).

APRIL

Amateur F.A. Cup Final at Wembley.
British Industries Fair at Earl's Court and Olympia (end of the month to first week of May).
Rugby League Cup Final at Wembley.

MAY

Chelsea Flower Show in Royal Hospital Grounds.
F.A. Cup Final at Wembley (beginning of the month).
London Fashion Fortnight (end of the month to beginning of June).
Opera Season begins at Royal Covent Garden Opera House.
Royal Academy Summer Exhibition opens at Burlington House.
Royal Windsor Horse Show at Windsor.

Antique Dealers' Fair at Grosvenor House.

Election of Sheriffs and other officers for City of London at the Guildhall (end of the month).

Eton and Harrow Match at Lord's (first week of the month).

The Oaks and the Derby at Epsom (first week of the month).

Richmond Royal Horse Show at Richmond.

Royal Ascot at Ascot (third week of the month).

Royal Tournament at Earl's Court.

Trooping the Colour (Queen's official birthday). At Horse Guards Parade.

Wimbledon Tennis Championships at Wimbledon.

JULY

A.A.A. Championships at the White City (mid-month).

Gentlemen *v.* Players at Lord's (mid-month).

Henley Royal Regatta at Henley.

International Horse Show at the White City.

Promenade Concerts at Royal Albert Hall begin.

Race for Doggett's Coat and Badge from London Bridge to Chelsea Bridge.

SEPTEMBER

Election of Lord Mayor at the Guildhall.

OCTOBER

Dairy Show at Olympia.

Horse of the Year Show at Harringay.

International Motor Show at Earl's Court.

NOVEMBER

Lord Mayor's Show. The new Lord Mayor drives in state through the City.

Memorial Ceremony at the Cenotaph.

State Opening of Parliament. The Queen drives in state from Buckingham Palace to the Houses of Parliament.

Chelsea Arts Ball at Royal Albert Hall.
Circuses open at Olympia, Harringay and Earl's Court (just before Xmas).
Oxford and Cambridge Rugby Match, at Twickenham.
Pantomimes open (Boxing Day).
Smithfield Show at Earl's Court.

ANTIQUES. London is the antique hunter's dream. Its hundreds of antique shops are bursting with everything from early Victorian chamber-pots to Fabergé Easter eggs. Those listed below are but a very few in the centre of London. If your tastes are less expensive, you will find the Portobello Road (running parallel with Ladbroke Grove), King's Road Chelsea, Church Street Kensington, and the Caledonian Market (now in Bermondsey Market behind London Bridge Station—Friday is the best day to go) good prospecting territory. The Antique Dealers' Association— to which all bigger reputable antique dealers belong—will help with advice if there is something special you want to find and can't. If you are in London while the Antique Dealers' Fair is on (June), try not to miss it. It's the best of its kind in the world.

Frederick Berry Ltd. 64 New Bond St. W1. Jewellery, *objets d'art*.

H. Blairman & Sons Ltd. 23 Grafton St. W1. Furniture, Chinese mirror pictures.

W. G. T. Burne, 27 Davies St. Berkeley Square, W1. Old English and Irish glass, chandeliers.

Cameo Corner, 26 Museum St. WC1. Antique jewellery.

Canterburys (Antiques) Ltd. 17 King St. St James's, SW1. Furniture, porcelain, works of art.

Delomosne and Son Ltd. 4 Campden Hill Rd. W8. Antique glass and porcelain.

C. Fredericks and Son, 76 Old Brompton Rd. SW7. Furniture.

Gered (Antiques) Ltd. 10 Piccadilly Arcade, SW1. Wedgwood specialists.

Goldsmiths & Silversmiths Co. Ltd. 112 Regent St. W1 English silver and jewellery.

Thomas Goode & Co. Ltd. 19 South Audley St. W1. China and glass.

H. R. Hancock & Sons, 37 Bury St. St James's, SW1. Old Chinese porcelain.

Loewenthal, 4 St James's St. SW1. Furniture (English 18th century), glass and silkwork pictures.

Thomas Lumley Ltd. 3 Bury St. St James's, SW1. Old silver.

Maggs Bros. Ltd. 50 Berkeley Square, W1. Antiquarian books and fine art.

Thomas H. Parker Ltd. 2 Albemarle St. W1. Maritime, military, sporting and historical pictures and prints.

Frank Partridge & Sons Ltd. 144–6 New Bond St. W1. English and French furniture.

Frank T. Sabin, Park House, 24 Rutland Gate, Knightsbridge, SW7. English, French, sporting paintings and engravings. Rowlandson drawings.

Chas. J. Sawyer Ltd. 12–13 Grafton St. W1. Fine art books.

Spink & Son Ltd. 5–7 King St. St James's, SW1. Jade, jewels, coins, pictures, oriental art.

Horace Walpole, 144 King's Rd. SW3.

APSLEY HOUSE [c5] Hyde Park Corner. Bears as its proud address 'No. 1, London'. A splendid Adam house, it was finished in 1778 and presented by Parliament to the first Duke of Wellington—the Iron Duke— in 1830. The present Duke has recently given it to the nation, together with the whole of its contents, as a Wellington  museum. It has been restored as far as possible to its original state, and is a magnificent example of period decoration. It holds a fascinating collection of Wellingtoniana and some fine old masters, including five Velasquez. It is open between 10 a.m. and 6 p.m. on weekdays, and between 2.30 and 6 p.m. on Sundays. You can walk along the Waterloo Gallery, look out on the old Duke's favourite view of Hyde Park, and see pretty well what he saw a hundred and twenty years ago.

ART GALLERIES. London is particularly rich in art galleries. Of the permanent public exhibitions (listed below) the National Gallery contains the nation's great traditional treasures; the Tate tends more towards modernity and holds great treasures of British art; the National Portrait Gallery, while containing some thoroughly bad pictures, is fascinating for its range of famous faces; and at Burlington House the Royal Academy has its Summer exhibition of what the Committee considers the best British art of the year.

Burlington House (Royal Academy) Piccadilly, W1. See daily press for details of exhibitions.   REG 4895

National Gallery, Trafalgar Square, WC2 Open weekdays, 10 a.m. to 6 p.m. Sundays 2 to 6 p.m. Admission free.   WHI 7618

National Portrait Gallery, St Martin's Place, WC2. Open weekdays Monday to Friday 11 a.m. to 5 p.m. Saturdays 11 a.m. to 6 p.m. Sundays 2 to 6 p.m. Admission free.   WHI 7611

Royal Academy Diploma Gallery, also at Burlington House. Weekdays 10 a.m. to 5.30 p.m. Sundays 2 to 5.30 p.m. Admission 2/-.

Tate Gallery, Millbank, SW1. British art and visiting collections. Open weekdays 10 a.m. to 6 p.m. Sundays 2 to 6 p.m. Admission free.   VIC 2556

Wallace Collection, Manchester Square, W1   WEL 0687

French paintings, furniture, porcelain, arms, etc. Open weekdays 10 a.m. to 5 p.m. Sundays 2 to 5 p.m. Admission free, except Tuesdays and Fridays—6d.

Whitechapel Art Gallery, Whitechapel High St. E1. Admission free. See daily press for details of exhibitions.   BIS 1492

As well as these public galleries, the private galleries listed below have, all the year round, exciting exhibitions of one kind or another, which are usually listed in the daily and the evening London press, as well as on Tube stations.

Adams Gallery, 92 New Bond St. W1	MAY 2468
Thomas Agnew, 43 Old Bond St. W1	REG 3042
Arts Council, 4 St James's Square, SW1	WHI 9737
Beaux Arts Gallery, 1 Bruton Place, W1	MAY 2573
Ben-Uri Jewish Art Gallery, 14 Portman St. W1	WEL 3001
Berkeley Galleries, 20 Davies St. W1	MAY 2450
P. & D. Colnaghi & Co. Ltd. 14 Old Bond St. W1	REG 1943
Fine Art Society, 148 New Bond St. W1	MAY 5116
Galerie Apollinaire, 3 Litchfield St. WC1	TEM 7413
Gimpel Fils, 50 South Molton St. W1	MAY 3720
Hanover Gallery, 32a St George St. W1	MAY 0296
Institute of Contemporary Arts, 17 Dover St. W1	GRO 6186
M. Knoedler & Co. Ltd. 14 Old Bond St. W1	REG 4238
Lefevre Galleries, 131 New Bond St. W1	MAY 2250
Leger Gallery, 13 Old Bond St. W1	REG 2679
Leicester Galleries, Leicester Square, WC2	WHI 3375
London Galleries, 23 Brook St. W1	MAY 6180
Marlborough Fine Art, 18 Old Bond St. W1	REG 6195
Parker Gallery, 2 Albemarle St. W1	REG 2785
Redfern Gallery, 20 Cork St. W1	REG 1732
Roland Browse & Delbanco, 19 Cork St. W1	REG 0804
Royal Society of British Artists Gallery, 6 Suffolk St. SW1	WHI 2828

Wildenstein & Co. Ltd. 147 New Bond St.
W1   MAY 0602
Zwemmer Gallery, 26 Litchfield St. WC1   TEM 1793

Open-air exhibitions are also annual events at Hampstead Heath (top of Heath St.) and Embankment Gardens, SW1.

ASCOT. See ANNUAL EVENTS and RACING.

AUCTION ROOMS. An auction in London is like an auction nowhere else. If you can spare the time, try and drop in to Christie's, Spencer House, 27 St James's Place, SW1 or Sotheby's, 34 New Bond Street, W1 or Phillips Son & Neale, 7 Blenheim Street, W1, which are all three in their own way perfect examples of the London auction-room atmosphere. Auctions are announced in the *Daily Telegraph* on Mondays, and *The Times* on Tuesdays. You can get catalogues in advance, and can usually inspect the lots three days beforehand. Be careful about nodding or moving your hands, or you'll find you've bought an umbrella stand, two Rembrandts and a shooting-box in Scotland.

AUTOMOBILE ASSOCIATION [E4] Head Office: Fanum House, New Coventry Street, W1 (WHI 1200). The A.A.'s services include patrols on all important main roads; over a thousand A.A. telephone boxes for members' free emergency calls; the supply of road maps and general information; the free A.A. handbook listing  hotels and garages; free legal representation; advice on insurance and temporary driving licences; free breakdown services, and so on. If you're coming from overseas, you can join at the Head Office or one of the provincial branches, or at the port of arrival. If you are a member of any of the A.A.'s linked overseas societies, you can get all the A.A. services free for six months of any one year.

B

BALLET. In recent years ballet has become enormously popular in London and there are now two permanent companies to choose from. One is to be seen at the Royal Opera House and the other at Sadler's Wells Theatre. The star company is the one at the Opera House, and its attractive little sister the one at the 'Wells'. Each company has a season devoted exclusively to ballet, as well as seasons when ballet alternates from night to night with opera. For programmes and times of performances see the newspapers.

BANK OF ENGLAND [H3 & 4] known familiarly as The Old Lady of Threadneedle Street, has stood where it is for two hundred and eighteen years, although five complete rebuildings have taken place, the last forbidding façade having been finished in 1941. The Bank was incorporated by Royal Charter in 1694. As a result of the Stuart depredations, it became a public company and remained so until its nationalisation in 1945. It is the only bank in England and Wales with the right to issue its own notes. It covers more than three acres, and is guarded every night by a detachment from the Brigade of Guards. Since 1780, when the Bank was thought to be in danger during the Gordon riots, the detachment has marched to the Bank every evening from Chelsea Barracks. The officer in charge of the detachment is allowed to entertain one male guest for dinner, so that if you happen to be a bank robber, the best thing to do is to strike up an acquaintance with a subaltern in the Guards. You can get into certain parts of the Bank and be shown around between 9 a.m. and 3 p.m. on weekdays.

BANKING HOURS, for all branches of all banks are:
    Weekdays: 10 a.m.–3 p.m.
    Saturdays: 10 a.m.–12 noon.

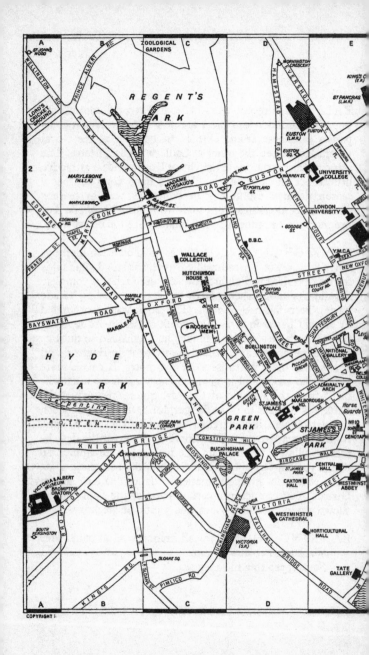

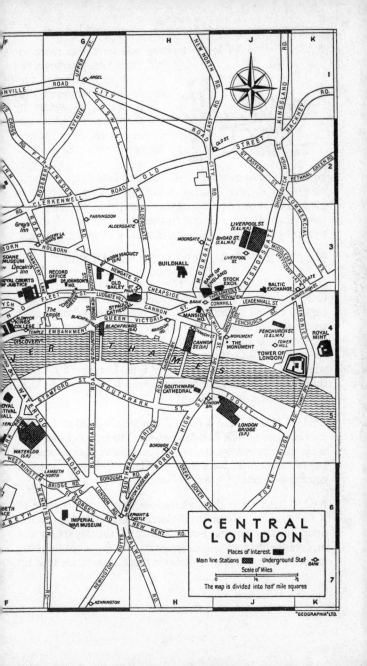

CENTRAL LONDON

Places of Interest ▨

Main line Stations ▨   Underground Stat ◇

Scale of Miles

0   ¼   ½

The map is divided into half mile squares

"GEOGRAPHIA" LTD.

BARROW BOY is the modern and somewhat more so-

phisticated counterpart of the Cockney costermonger, recognisable in summer by his smart braces, in winter by his drape-cut overcoat, and all the year round by the nervous glance over the shoulder to see if there's a copper coming. The barrow boys sell fruit and flowers from irregular pitches all over London. Nowadays, only a few of them give short weight or short change since, as a fraternity, they have discovered, somewhat to their shocked bewilderment, that they can make quite a lot of money by being honest.

BATTERSEA. See PLEASURE GARDENS.

B.B.C. [D3] Broadcasting House, the British Broadcasting Corporation's headquarters, stands at the Portman Square end of Regent Street, the big white building that looks like a ship. Famous faces pass in and out at the rate of about one a minute. You can get tickets to see certain B.B.C. shows while you are in London by writing to: The Ticket Unit, B.B.C. London W1, three weeks in advance of the showing, enclosing a stamped addressed envelope.

BED AND BREAKFAST can be obtained in literally tens of thousands of London houses. The bed and breakfast areas spread out around all main line railway stations and are largest around Victoria and Paddington. A good average price is between 15/- and 21/- a night.

BELGRAVIA is the area enclosed within the triangle of Knightsbridge, Hyde Park Corner and Victoria, centred upon Belgrave Square. Few of its large houses, as stately and mellow as a nineteenth-century politician after a good dinner, are still run as private residences. Most of them are split up into flats or used as clubs or Embassy buildings. The smart people now tend to live in the mews with which the region is honeycombed. It's still an airy and gracious part of London to walk through and gives the best unspoilt impression of upper-class living fifty years ago.

BERKELEY SQUARE, W1 [C & D 4] has never recovered its pre-war grace since A Nightingale Sang there above the hastily-dug shelters in 1940. Once surrounded by aristocratic houses, it is now almost entirely a business area. In the spring, the daffodils in the ragged grass under the trees still have a charm which the well-tailored flowers of its tidier neighbour, Grosvenor Square, never can achieve.

BIG BEN [E5] strictly the name of the great bell (named after Sir Benjamin Hall, Commissioner of Works when it

was hung) is now used by everyone to apply to the Clock Tower and Clock itself of the Palace of Westminster. Its warm avuncular boom is the most famous of any bell in the world. Year after year, thousands of visitors try to get into the Clock Tower; but no one is allowed in. The reason is that the movement and disturbance caused might upset the works. When the lantern on the balcony above the Tower is lit, it means that Parliament is sitting.

BILLINGSGATE MARKET [J4]. The time to see London's fish-market (it has borne its present name for a thousand years or more) is soon after it has opened at 5.30 in the morning. To 'talk Billingsgate' means to swear hideously and constantly. But the present-day porters—all men —claim that this is a libel and that the bad language left the Market when the last fishwives left. Go there on a workmen's Tube to London Bridge, and listen for yourself one day before breakfast—there's a pub there called the *King's Head and Mermaid* (116 Lower Thames Street) which opens at 7 a.m.

BLOOMSBURY, WC1. The area surrounding the British Museum and embracing the clean pale modern buildings of London University is still—while steadily losing ground to Chelsea—the home of students, artists, poets, journalists. Its association with the arts goes back to the eighteenth century, and in the nineteenth, William Morris, Shelley, Coleridge, Swinburne, Macaulay, Thackeray, Burne-Jones, Dickens, Hazlitt and Lamb all lived there at one time or another. It contains a number of sound, cheap hotels, a good sprinkling of bookshops, some charming tree-filled squares, and is, incidentally, the publishing centre of London.

BOAT RACE. The race between the Oxford and Cambridge Universities' Eights from Putney to Mortlake every March, which has been going on since the middle of the last century (Cambridge are slightly ahead), is, in terms of the numbers of people who watch it—two to three hundred thousand on a fine day—London's most popular sporting event. You watch it on the tow path, or from one of the bridges—Hammersmith Bridge is a great favourite—there are no stands or enclosures of any kind. Don't miss it if you're in London on Boat Race Day. But tread carefully in Piccadilly Circus on Boat Race Night.

BOBBY (after Sir Robert Peel, founder of the Metropolitan Police Force) is the commonest London slang term for a policeman. It is *not* derogatory, as are 'copper' and 'rozzer'. 'Constable' or 'Officer' are the polite forms of address.

BOND STREET [D4] is famous for its art galleries, smart shops and its even smarter pedestrian traffic. Linking

Piccadilly with Oxford Street, it is Mayfair's main shopping
artery. To see it at its best, stroll along it just before
lunch on a sunny morning (walking is anyway quicker
than riding at that time) and pick out the model
girls with their square make-up boxes tripping
along to a date with that nice textile manufacturer;
clubmen with their umbrellas and bowler hats
strolling towards St James's and the Mall; art
critics dropping into Wildenstein's for a quick
look round; housewives from Beckenham window-
shopping; bankers popping into Sulka's to order a dozen
shirts; typists letting off steam, and people like you and me
just walking up and down.

BOOKMAKERS. You can open a credit account with
any one of a thousand bookmakers in London. Of the many,
perhaps the four best-known are:

David Cope Ltd. Ludgate Circus, EC4	CEN 4272
Wm. Hill Ltd. Hill House, W1	WHI 3422
Ladbroke & Co. Ltd. 6 Old Burlington St. W1	REG 6700
Douglas Stuart, 6 Brook St. W1	GRO 7000

You can also bet off the course with the tote by using

Tote Investors Ltd. 3 Ridinghouse St. W1	LAN 6666

BOOKS. London abounds in bookshops that are remarkable both for the wide range of their stocks and for the high
level of helpfulness and knowledge that you are liable to
encounter among the assistants. For second-hand books, a
stroll down Charing Cross Road, stacked with (literally)
millions of them, will take you a whole day once you start
browsing. It's invidious to single out just a few; excellent
bookshops are found throughout London, and in nearly all
big stores.

BOOKSTALLS. W. H. Smith & Son (Wyman's at Paddington and Euston) have bookstalls at most railway stations, airports, many hotels and Tube stations.

BOWLER HAT. The possession of the correct type of bowler, hairy, not too large and curly-brimmed, is as essential to the young man about town as a pair of trousers. It is worn either in the hand which is not carrying the rolled umbrella, or, sometimes, even on the head, tilted forward over the eyes at the angle adopted by villains in Victorian melodrama. The most London of all headgear; for where and how to buy them, see SHOPPING—HATS.

BOXING AND WRESTLING. The big fights take  place at Harringay, the White City or the Albert Hall. Smaller cards are staged at a number of local arenas. Among these, perhaps the best for an evening's entertainment is the Bethnal Green Baths (Central Line Tube to Bethnal Green). For details, see the London evening press.

BRITISH TRAVEL AND HOLIDAYS ASSOCIATION [D5] Queen's House, 64–65 St James's Street, SW1 (MAY 9191) is the official company whose job it is to attract tourists to this country and to look after them while they're here. Unlike many tourist offices, it's a highly efficient and wide-awake Association which is ready and waiting to serve you.  There you will get a straightforward answer to any question you want to ask. The B.T.H.A. issues a hotel guide; information booklets on all aspects of British life; an excellent monthly magazine called *Coming Events*, and an information sheet about London hotels. They will also arrange, if you want it, private accommodation in people's homes, or can, for example, recommend one of their two hundred and seven guides or lecturers who are registered with the Association and are available for visitors.

BUCKINGHAM PALACE [D5]. The London residence of the Queen began its life in the seventeenth century as a mulberry garden planted by James I, who had ideas about promoting a native silk industry. The Duke of Buckingham built a house on the site, which remained there until 1825, when Nash redesigned it and its name was changed from 'House' to 'Palace'. Queen Victoria was the first monarch to take up residence there and it has developed bit by bit since that time, the façade being completed in its present form just before World War I. When the Queen is in residence the Royal Standard is flown. You see the Palace best from the end of the Mall with Carlton House Terrace on the one side and St James's Park on the other. The Palace is never open to the public, but you can go and look through the railings, take photographs of the sentries, and in the morning, if you are lucky, see the Changing of the Guard (see CHANGING OF THE GUARD).

BURLINGTON ARCADE [D4] Piccadilly, W1. If you run, play a musical instrument or put up your umbrella in the Arcade, you will be politely but sternly requested to desist by one of the beadles. For this oldest of all shopping arcades, practically unchanged in appearance for the last one hundred and thirty-five years or so (except at the Burlington Gardens end, where a bomb cocked a snook at the beadle during World War II), believes in tradition. Some of the loveliest old shops in London are there (see SHOPPING). You will be warned of closing time by the ringing of the old brass bell in the middle of the Arcade. A stroll past the shop windows is a perfect way to pass a rainy ten minutes.

BURLINGTON HOUSE [D4] Piccadilly, W1 shelters behind its splendid portals a whole pride of learned societies, which includes the Society of Antiquaries, the Royal

Society, the Geological, the Astronomical and Linnean. It also houses the Royal Academy (see ART GALLERIES).

BUSES. The big red buses of the London Transport Executive,  besides achieving a million miracles a day in terms of traffic negotiation, go everywhere cheaply, safely and—unless they are ahead of schedule —surprisingly quickly. Their drivers, who, as a body, conduct a permanent running fight with the drivers of taxis, are supernaturally good. Their conductors and conductresses (known as clippies) are an unfailing source of Cockney humour which ranges from the jovially benign to the acidly destructive. Shortest ride 2d. GREEN LINE buses go on longer routes out into the Home Counties and have different stopping points. Details of their routes can be found in Tube stations or can be got from the London Transport Executive, 55 Broadway, SW1 (ABB 1234).

C

CAR AIR FERRY SERVICE. Silver City Airways Ltd. 1 Great Cumberland Place, W1 (PAD 7040) operate a car air ferry service to the Continent, and will give you full details of their service if you telephone them.

CAR HIRE. You can hire cars to drive yourself, or with driver, by the hour or day or week. Rates are fairly general and vary according to the size of the car. I can strongly recommend Welbeck Motors Ltd. 107 Crawford Street, W1 (WEL 3991) and the Daimler Hire Co. Ltd. 243 Knightsbridge, SW7 (SLO 3456), from both of whom I have always had excellent service. Another thoroughly reliable firm is Godfrey Davis Ltd. 7 Eccleston Street, SW1 (SLO 0022).

If you come from abroad, the Automobile Association will tell you how to get a temporary driving licence (see AUTOMOBILE ASSOCIATION).

CARLYLE'S HOUSE, 24 Cheyne Row, Chelsea, SW3. The house in which Thomas Carlyle lived for the last thirty-eight years of his life has been kept exactly as he left it. A fascinating period piece, it does more perhaps to keep Carlyle's memory alive today than his writing. It's open on weekdays from ten in the morning until dusk in the winter, and six o'clock in the summer.

CAVELL, Nurse Edith [E4] St Martin's Place. The bleak and formalised statue of Nurse Edith Cavell ('Patriotism is not enough') who was executed by the Germans in World War I, stands between Trafalgar Square and Charing Cross Road. It has come in for a lot of criticism; but at least it's dignified.

CENOTAPH [E5]. Designed by Sir Edwin Lutyens, the simple and austere national memorial to the dead of the Commonwealth in both world wars stands in the middle of Whitehall. It's the focal point of the nation's mourning on Remembrance Day. Men raise their hats when they pass it.

CHANGING OF THE GUARD takes place (in theory —but times are subject to alteration and the weather) at Buckingham Palace every other morning between 10.30 and 11.30. The ceremony is at its best when the Queen is in residence and the Guard at its full strength. Other Guard-changing ceremonies take place at St James's Palace, and in Horse Guards Parade—the first at the same time as Buckingham Palace on the even days of the month, the second every weekday at 11 a.m. and at 10 on Sundays. They always attract large crowds, so go early if you want to make sure of getting a good place in the front, where you can see and take photographs.

CHARING CROSS ROAD, WC2 [E3 & 4] is the headquarters of second-hand bookselling, music publishing and American-style tailoring. It's a fascinating street to wander along, from the Irving Statue at the Trafalgar Square end, over Cambridge Circus, and up to its traffic-jammed junction with Oxford Street.

CHARLES I [E5] Whitehall. One of the genuinely fine statues of London (by Hubert le Sueur), it was cast in 1663, but not put up until after the Restoration in 1674, having happily not been destroyed, as was planned, during the Commonwealth. There was a lot of fuss about renovating it in the nineteenth century, which was finally squashed by Lord Esher in 1900; so that we are, for once, left with the original statue on its original pedestal.

CHELSEA, long famous as the home of artists, London's nearest approach to a Latin Quarter, is now the favourite area of civil servants and business men as well. An attractive and friendly place, which centres round the King's Road and runs from Sloane Square down to the river, it's studded with some very good cheapish restaurants, antique shops, drinking clubs. Both its men and women wear corduroy trousers. It also houses the Chelsea Football Club (at Stamford Bridge), long known as 'poor old Chelsea', the despair and the delight—mostly the former—of its supporters.

CHELSEA FLOWER SHOW. The annual show of the

Royal Horticultural Society is held in May in the grounds of the—

CHELSEA ROYAL HOSPITAL. Completed by Wren in 1692, it houses the famous Chelsea Pensioners (often confused with the football team), who change from their dark blue winter coats to their better-known long red summer coats on Oak Apple Day (29th May), Charles II's birthday, in honour of his early support of the Hospital. In a walk up the King's Road, you will always see one or more of these old soldiers resolutely not fading away. The Hospital gardens are open from March to October from nine in the morning till dusk.

CHEMISTS. Boots The Chemists, and Timothy Whites & Taylors have branches throughout London, and are completely reliable. All-night and Sunday-opening chemists are:

Boots The Chemists, 219 Piccadilly,   GER 8246
W1
Boots The Chemists, 25 Aldgate   BIS 9979
High St. EC3
John Bell & Croyden, 50 Wigmore   WEL 5555
St. W1

CHINA AND GLASS. Fine china and glass are to be found everywhere in London, with an emphasis on the fine chinaware and earthenware that have been coming out of the Potteries of Staffordshire for the last two hundred years and more. Below are just a few of the shops worth visiting.

The General Trading Co. (Mayfair), 1–5 Grantham Place (at the Piccadilly end of Park Lane). Table china and glass, expensive.

Gered, 10 Piccadilly Arcade, W1. Biggest dealers in antique Wedgwood in the world.

Goode's, 19 South Audley St. W1. Antique and modern. Famous and expensive.

J. Rochelle Thomas, 14 King St. W1. Antique china of the grandest sort.

The Royal Copenhagen Porcelain Co. 5 Old Bond St. W1. Danish porcelain and glass.

John Sparks, 128 Mount St. W1. A wide selection of antique china; specialist in Chinese porcelain.

The Venetian Glass Galleries, 81 Knightsbridge, SW1 for Venetian ware.

The Wedgwood Showrooms, 34 Wigmore St. W1. Wedgwood, antique and modern. Don't miss the museum.

For everyday table-ware, try the big stores, or *Lawley's*, 154 Regent St. W1.

CHURCHES. London is sprinkled with churches, lovely and ugly, old and new, white stone and red brick, serenley spired or roofed with corrugated iron. Church of England churches are everywhere; and there are plenty of Nonconformist and Catholic churches too. There's a list below of other kinds of places of worship in or around the West End of London. Sir Christopher Wren, to whom the Great Fire of London in 1666 came as a godsend rather than a disaster, built some of the loveliest churches in the world, most of them in the City. Although many were damaged during the Blitz, enough of them still stand to leave him a perpetual memorial. (For details, see WREN CHURCHES.)

Baptist

Bloomsbury Central Church, Shaftesbury Avenue, WC2
Kingsgate, Southampton Row, WC1

Christian Science

First Church, Sloane Terrace, SW1
Third Church, Curzon St. W1
Eleventh Church, Nutford Place, Bryanston Square, W1

Church of Scotland

Crown Court, Drury Lane, WC2

Congregational

King's Weigh House Church, Duke St. Grosvenor Square, W1
Orange St. Leicester Square, WC2
Paddington, Marylebone Rd. NW1
Westminster Congregational Chapel, Buckingham Gate, SW1

Dutch

The Dutch Church, Austin Friars, EC2

French Protestant

French Evangelical Reformed Church, Monmouth Rd. Bayswater
French Protestant Huguenot Church of London, 8 Soho Square, W1

German

St Georgs Kirche, Alie St. Whitechapel.

Greek Orthodox Church

St Sophia, Moscow Rd. Bayswater, W2

Jewish

Great Synagogue, Duke's Place, EC3
Central Synagogue, Great Portland St. W1
West London Reform Synagogue, Upper Berkeley St. W1

Methodist

Central Hall, Westminster, SW1
Kingsway Hall, Kingsway, WC1
Methodist Church, Hinde St. W1

Russian Orthodox Church

St Philip, 188 Buckingham Palace Rd. SW1

Salvation Army
275 Oxford St. W1

Society of Friends
Meeting House, Euston Rd. NW1

Swiss Protestant
Swiss Church of London, 79 Endell St. Long Acre, WC2

Unitarian
London Domestic Mission, 28 Bell St. Edgware Rd. NW1

By the way, there's a charming little Children's Church attached to Ealing Green Congregational Church (near Ealing Broadway Tube Station), which children run themselves under an adult chairman. Children's services are held there every Sunday morning.

CINEMAS. You'll find the programmes and times of showing of films at West End cinemas in the classified columns of the evening papers. For a fuller guide (including suburban cinemas) get WHAT'S ON IN LONDON, 6d. every Friday (which is, incidentally, a useful little guide to theatres and concerts and the week's events in general). You can smoke in cinemas and do not have to tip the attendants. All programmes are continuous, unless otherwise advertised.

CIRCUSES only come to London at Christmas. The top two are Bertram Mills' Circus at Olympia—the aristocrat of the circus world—and Tom Arnold's Circus at Harringay. They still smell of horses and sawdust and oranges. If you are in London at circus-time you should book well ahead. With the years, they seem to be losing none of their dash or colour or appeal.

CITY, The. The City has been proudly independent since 886 when King Alfred used his influence to make his son-in-law an alderman. It still has its Court of Common Council, consisting of the Lord Mayor, twenty-five aldermen and two hundred and six commoners, with its headquarters in Guildhall, which was built in 1411 (see GUILDHALL). It has, too, its own police force, recognisable by a helmet with a crest-like ridge instead of the ordinary silver knob on top, and a red and white striped brassard instead of blue and white. When you see constables dressed like this, you know you're in the City.

Prominent in the affairs of the City are the Guilds, originally trade defence organisations, now largely philanthropic institutions, whose members do not necessarily have anything to do with the trade the Guild once protected. The Queen is a Draper, for example, and the Duke of Edinburgh a Fishmonger. Some of the old trade names are still commemorated: Armourers and Brasiers, Broderers, Cordwainers, Curriers, Fanmakers, Farriers, Fletchers, Girdlers, Horners, Loriners, Paviors, Poulters, Tallow Chandlers, Upholders.

Some of the Halls of the Guilds—or City Livery Companies as they're called—are magnificent in pillared loftiness and gold leaf. You can write to those listed below if you want to see over them. In keeping with their stateliness, Clerks of the Halls like to have a little notice of your visit.

Apothecaries' Hall, 14 Black Friars Lane, EC4
Butchers' Hall, 87 & 88 Bartholomew Close, EC1
Cutlers' Hall, 4 Warwick Lane, Newgate St. EC4
Drapers' Hall, Throgmorton St. EC2
Dyers' Hall, 10 Dowgate Hill, EC4
Fishmongers' Hall, London Bridge, EC4
Goldsmiths' Hall, Foster Lane, EC2

Grocers' Hall, Princes St. EC2

Ironmongers' Hall, Shaftesbury Place, Aldersgate St. EC1

Merchant Taylors' Hall, 30 Threadneedle St. EC2

Painter Stainers' Hall, 9 Little Trinity Lane, EC4

Skinners' Hall, 8 Dowgate Hill, EC4

Stationers' Hall, Ludgate Hill, EC4

Vintners' Hall, 68 Upper Thames St. EC4

Watermen and Lightermen's Hall, 18 St Mary-at-Hill, EC3 .

The City has two faces: its weekday and its week-end face. During the week it's one of the busiest square miles of the world, its narrow streets jammed with traffic, its pavements crowded. But go there on Sunday morning; take a Tube to the Bank and you'll find yourself in a ghost town. Threadneedle Street and Throgmorton Street and Lombard Street are dead and echoing. An occasional lonely taxi can be heard a quarter of a mile off. For hardly anyone lives in the City; the days when the great merchants kept palaces there are long since gone. Now it's just a place to work in; and on Sunday it sleeps.

CITY GUILDS. See CITY, The.

CLARENCE HOUSE [D5] St James's, SW1. Originally built by John Nash for the Duke of Clarence, its enlargement in 1875 ruined the original architecturally. It was formerly the residence of the Queen, but is not at the moment occupied by Royalty.

CLEANING AND PRESSING. Out of hundreds of dry cleaners in London (and the Burtol and Achille Serre chains are always reliable) I can personally recommend the Berkeley Cleaners at 50 Curzon Street (GRO 2129), and Lilliman and Cox at 35 Bruton Place, Berkeley Square (MAY 4555). Most cleaners also operate valet services.

CLEOPATRA'S NEEDLE [F4] Victoria Embankment. Brought to London in 1777, it was originally an obelisk dedicated to the Sun God by Thothmes III fifteen hundred years before the birth of Christ. Its brothers stand in the Place de la Concorde, Paris, and Central Park, New York. The chips and scratches on its surface are the newest things about it—the result of enemy bombs.

CLUBS. Since the days when the palaces of Pall Mall and St James's were no more than coffee houses, where a regular clientele met every morning to discuss the latest Cabinet or the latest cuckold, the clubs of London have had a wide and powerful influence on Britain's affairs. Exclusive, and for men only, among their few thousands of members are numbered all the important officials of Church and State, leaders of thought in every sphere and most of the hereditary aristocracy. The last one hundred and fifty years or so have seen the development of specific club types: the Savage has a hard-drinking Bohemian tradition; the Athenaeum nearby, resounds to the lofty neo-platonism of Bishops and dons; in Buck's and Boodle's and White's the blue blood is even thicker than the carpets; in the Junior Carlton a great number of middle-aged business men talk medium-important business; the Garrick has been the scene of a wedding between the stage and the bar; chotah-pegs disappear beneath grizzled moustaches with military precision at the Army and Navy; diplomats and senior civil servants tipple discreetly at the Travellers'; Cabinet Ministers past and present are ten-a-penny at the St James's and Brooks's. Membership at the thirty or so clubs which matter, costs, on an average, fifteen to twenty guineas a year, after you have paid your entrance fee of about the same amount. You have, of course, to be correctly proposed, seconded and supported to be elected to a club. The advantages? Over and above the residential facilities, the good food and wine and the large arm-chairs to sleep in after lunch, it's the talk—and the friendships which are made—that really matter.

Besides these venerable and exclusive establishments there are a few clubs open to everyone that are particularly useful for visitors. Some of them have (fairly limited) residential accommodation; you can eat there reasonably; above all, you can meet people. Below are just one or two of them. In each case, you should write to the Secretary for further information:

English-Speaking Union, 37 Charles St. WI   MAY 7400
National Book League (non-residential), 7
Albemarle St. WI.   REG 1201
Overseas League (Members must support
the tenets of the League), Overseas House,
St James's, SWI   REG 5051
Victoria League (non-residential), 38 Chesham Place, SWI.   SLO 6101

COACHES. Britain is covered by a network of coach systems which, while being rather slower, are cheaper than trains. Telephone SLO 0202, Victoria Coach Station, SWI for information about routes and fares.

COCKNEY. The Cockney—strictly defined as someone born within the sound of Bow Bells—has come loosely to mean a Londoner. The true Cockney breed, small, tough, chirpy, resilient and adaptive, has much in common with the house sparrows that scurry and quarrel and joke on a million London rooftops. As a pure strain, with its own language and customs, its own tribal morality and dress, its own laws and logic, the breed is dying out, as longer education and the wide dissemination of a neutral accent by the B.B.C. and films, have their effect.

The Cockney character was moulded in the slums of a

London which is slowly disappearing. New housing estates are springing up in the heart of the Cockney districts—in Poplar and Bermondsey and Bethnal Green and Stepney—and as the elements which created it disappear, so the Cockney character tends to merge with the middle classes and become lost. The language too is dying out; the accent is less defined than it was; and rhyming slang, originally a thieves' *argot* bred in the stews and taverns of the London of *The Beggers' Opera*, is dying out too. Rhyming slang works on a simple principle, but it can be absolutely baffling to the uninitiated. A cup of tea, for example, becomes 'a cup of Rosie Lee', which in turn loses the last rhyming syllable and becomes simply 'a cup of Rosie'. Thus, stairs ('apples and pears') become 'apples'; feet ('plates of meat') 'plates'. Some phrases are never shortened; also the rhyme follows the true pronunciation; thus: water—'baked potater'; wife—'trouble and strife'; window (pronounced 'winder')—'burnt cinder'; beer—'pig's ear'. It's a unique and fascinating language. Let's hope it lives on. An encouraging sign (which shows that it's still alive) is that the old phrase for a gin, 'a barrel and pin', has been ousted in recent years in favour of 'a Vera Lynn'.

COMMONWEALTH OFFICES

Australia	Australia House, Aldwych, WC2	TEM 6611
New South Wales	56 Strand, WC2	TRA 7477
Queensland	409 Strand, WC2	TEM 3224
South Australia	499 Oxford St. W1	MAY 5061
Victoria	Victoria House, Melbourne Place, WC2	TEM 2656
Canada	Canada House, Trafalgar Square, SW1	WHI 9741
Ceylon	13 Hyde Park Gardens, W2	AMB 1841
India	India House, Aldwych, WC2	TEM 8484

New Zealand	415 Strand, WC2	TEM 3241
Northern Ireland	13 Regent St. SW1	WHI 0651
Northern Rhodesia	57 Haymarket, SW1	WHI 2040
Pakistan	34 Lowndes Square, SW1	SLO 3402
South Africa	South Africa House, Trafalgar Square, WC2	WHI 4488
Southern Rhodesia	429 Strand, WC2	TEM 1133

CONSULATES. Addresses are given in the Telephone Directory under the names of the different countries.

CORONATION CHAIR. The Chair in which monarchs are crowned is in Westminster Abbey. The Stone of Scone, brought back by Edward I from Scotland, and lifted in the dead of night by Scottish Nationalists in 1951 and missing for some months, is now tucked safely underneath the seat again.

COUNTY HALL [F5] Westminster Bridge, SE1. The large beige-coloured modern building (it was completed in 1933) on the other side of the river opposite the Houses of Parliament, is the headquarters of the London County Council. The main entrance is in Belvedere Road. On alternate Tuesdays at 2.30, you can listen to the one hundred and fifty Council members discussing the affairs of the capital. The public gallery is small; and the best thing to do if you want to see over County Hall, or to attend a Council meeting, is to get in touch with the Clerk of the Council.

COVENT GARDEN [E4] is London's fruit, vegetable and flower market. A noisy nerve-racking place very early in the morning, by mid-day it fades into sleepiness and an underfoot mush of cabbage leaves and rotten apples. Its porters perform prodigies of balance with tiers of baskets, which they carry on their heads. Go there at six o'clock on a sunny summer morning—although half the market's working day is already over, you will still find plenty going on and the best free flower show in the world. There are plenty of pubs round the market which open early. My favourite is the *White Swan*, New Row, Covent Garden, which opens at 5 a.m. Arising from the petunias and potatoes is the ROYAL COVENT GARDEN OPERA HOUSE [E4] where London's top opera and ballet functions take place. During the Season, it's a common thing to see dukes and dowagers in white tie and tails and tiaras walking through the narrow stall-cluttered streets of the market (impossible to park in) towards the Opera House in broad daylight—a favourite subject for cartoonists.

CRICKET. The world headquarters of the game is the Marylebone Cricket Club (the M.C.C.) at Lord's. This most dignified and gracious of grounds (see LORD'S) is well worth a visit. For a warmer and less respectful day's play, go to the Oval (see OVAL) across the river, the Surrey Club's headquarters.

CROWN JEWELS. The fabulous Crown Jewels (including a huge ruby which belonged to the Black Prince, pearl earrings worn by Elizabeth I, and all the incomparable State regalia of orb, crown and sceptre) are kept in a kind of aquarium at the Tower of London. And there, through thick bars, behind a railing, and under the kindly eye of a yeoman warder, you can look at them; for the Tower has never quite forgotten Colonel Blood (no relation to Errol Flynn) and his seventeenth-century companions, who got halfway out of the Tower with the Jewels. But the Keeper's son, arriving home unexpectedly, thought there was something suspicious about the bulging cloaks of the gallant gentlemen, and raised the alarm.

CRUFT'S DOG SHOW. See ANNUAL EVENTS.

D

DANCE HALLS. If you like dancing (or feel lonely) there are a number of dance halls which are open, often in the afternoon, always in the evenings. Most of them serve drinks, and all of them light refreshments. Among the most popular are:

Astoria Salon, 165 Charing Cross Rd. WC2	GER	1711
Hammersmith Palais, 7 Brook Green Rd. W6	RIV	2812
Lyceum, Wellington St. WC2	TEM	3715
Paramount, Tottenham Court Rd. W1	EUS	4173

DEBUTANTES. As the last daffodils bend their heads, so the 'debs' raise theirs. Much less publicised in post-war years, the debutante of today quite often works for a living, and can usually be recognised at the *Berkeley* or *Quag's* or the *Four Hundred* by the loudness of her voice and the pinkness of her escort. A large part of the London Season is built around the coming-out dances given for debutantes by fond papas, and which are still splendid events. To see 'debs' at their best and in bulk, go to the Eton and Harrow Match at Lord's.

DELICATESSENS. If you are staying with friends or in rooms and want to buy something at an improbable time or on a Sunday—something tasty like a ripe Camembert or some ham or salami or any of the staples—you will find *Schmidt's* at 41 Charlotte Street, W1, open until 10.30 p.m. every day. I can also thoroughly recommend *Leon's* at 7 Marylebone High Street, W1, which is open on Saturday afternoons, and until 12.30 p.m. on Sundays. Brewer

Street and Old Compton Street in Soho contain a number of delicatessens, many of them with special Continental importations. Two that I like are the *Little Pulteney Stores* in Brewer Street and *Gomez Ortega* in Old Compton Street.

DERBY. See RACING and ANNUAL EVENTS.

DICKENS' LONDON. Much of London has changed almost beyond recognition since Dickens filled it with the people of his imagination. But many associations still remain. In Portsmouth Street (leading from Portugal Street to Lincoln's Inn Fields) the Old Curiosity Shop still does well on the strength of those associations. Visitors to the *George and Vulture* in Castle Court, off Cornhill, still ask to see the room that Mr Pickwick occupied while he waited for his case to come to Court. In the Strand you can still see the Roman bath where David Copperfield took a plunge. *Jack Straw's Castle* still caters to Londoners enjoying the air of Hampstead Heath, as it did when Mrs Bardell was arrested there taking a dish of tea. Bill Sikes and Nancy would still be able to find their way about through Smithfield along Little Britain down to London Bridge and into the Borough.

A major effort by the Dickens Fellowship has converted 48 Doughty Street in Bloomsbury—where *Oliver Twist*, *The Pickwick Papers* and *Nicholas Nickleby* were written—into a Dickens Museum and Library, containing the table at which he was writing just before his death, and a wonderful collection of Dickensiana. In the basement has been reproduced the kitchen of Dingley Dell where Mr Pickwick caused so much jollity with the servants on that never-to-be-forgotten Christmas. The Museum is open from 10 to 12.30 and from 2 to 5. Closed on Sundays. Admission 1/-.

DINING CLUBS. Over the past few years a number of lunching and dining clubs have sprung up in London, catering for the customer who wants really good food, a *chic* atmosphere, and is ready to spend a lot of money.

There's usually no nonsense about election to membership —you simply write in, find yourself proposed and seconded immediately, and receive a membership card as soon as you've paid your subscription. Most clubs make special terms for people who are in London for only a short time. Don't expect to pay less than about 25/- a head, plus wine, for lunch, and about 35/- a head for dinner. With drinks and tips, an evening for two costs you anything between £4 and £10, depending on the size and number of your drinks and the cost of what you eat. Listed below is my own choice of the better known clubs.

Albany, 3 Savile Row, W1 (REG 7382). Headquarters of sportsmen and variety people. Dining and cabaret in the downstairs restaurant.

Les Ambassadeurs, 5 Hamilton Place, W1 (GRO 6555). Favourite of film and stage people and always full after glossy premieres and first nights. Delightful garden bar and open-air eating in the summer. The entrance fee and the annual subscription also take care of the Milroy— famous war-time night club, now on the floor above *Les Ambee* (as everyone calls it). Two bands. No cabaret.

Bon Viveur, 52 Hertford St. W1 (GRO 1175) concentrates on good food. Quiet little place, in Shepherd Market with a gay South of France décor. Pleasant small bar.

The Empress, 35 Dover St. W1 (REG 8100). Once famous as a residential club for women, now one of the gayer night spots. You dine to soft music in the Persian Room, and dance in the Crystal Room.

The Gargoyle, 69 Dean St. W1 (GER 6455). Once the haunt of every Bohemian with the price of a drink in his corduroys, the Gargoyle is quieter now, with only occasional eruptions into its former liveliness. You can eat and dance as cheaply there as anywhere in London— from 8.30 p.m. onwards.

Le Petit Club Français, 4 St James's Place, SW1 (REG 5440). An intimate and inexpensive lunch and dining club. Good food and cellar. Open after the theatre.

La Rue, 20 Queen St. Mayfair, W1 (MAY 5985). Smart luncheon and dining club with meals on the roof garden during the summer. No music. Favourite with visiting Americans.

Siegi's, 46 Charles St. Mayfair, W1 (GRO 1360). Bar and restaurant popular with columnists and show business people. No music.

The 21 Room, 8 Chesterfield Gardens, W1 (GRO 1710). An Edwardian dandy in buttoned satin with candelabra. Large, comfortable bar. Dining garden for the summer. Dancing to two bands. Cabaret.

DISCOVERY, The, [F4] moored below Waterloo Bridge took Captain Scott to the South Pole. Now a training vessel for Sea Scouts, it houses a fascinating museum of Scott relics. Open weekdays 2 p.m. to 4.30 p.m. Saturdays 10 a.m. to 2.30 p.m. Admission 1/-. Children 6d.

DOCKS. The Port of London Authority runs cruises along the Docks during the summer months. You can get details from the Senior Information Officer, Dock Cruises, P.L.A., Trinity Square, EC3 (ROY 2000). Much of London's wealth has sprung from the thousands of acres of wharves and cranes and railway lines which sprawl from below Woolwich up to Tower Bridge (see also RIVER BUSES).

DOCTORS AND DENTISTS. Under the National Health Scheme, treatment by doctors and at hospitals is free. The most you have to pay a dentist (except for dentures) is £1. There are still, particularly in London, a number of doctors and dentists who haven't joined the Scheme, where the old system of consultation by appointment for varying fees still applies; but these are the exceptions rather than the rule.

If you need a doctor or a dentist while you're in London, it's quite simple. As an out-of-town visitor, you go to the nearest post office and ask for the address of the local Executive Council, which will then fix you up with a doctor or a dentist. If you're from overseas, you do exactly the same, but you must produce your passport. If you're staying in the country for more than three months, you should apply to Insurance House, Insurance Street, WCI (TER 2266)—ask for the Enquiry Office—for a temporary National Insurance number.

In a case of emergency, you can always go direct to the out-patients department of any large hospital. Most people will be able to tell you where the nearest one is. Taxi drivers and policemen are always particularly helpful on occasions like this. If there's a really serious emergency, dial 999 on the nearest telephone.

DOWNING STREET, SW1 [E5] takes its name, ironically enough, from a notorious political opportunist, Sir George Downing, who became a fervent Republican when Cromwell came to power, and a Royalist again during the Restoration. The Prime Minister lives at Number 10, whose impassively ordinary front door guards the nation's secrets. The Chancellor of the Exchequer lives at Number 11, and the Chief Government Whip at Number 12. Downing Street fills up at times of crisis or on occasions like Budget Day, but most of the time it's as quiet as any Westminster side street. See for yourself, by strolling from the Houses of Parliament along Whitehall and taking the second turning on the left.

DUKE OF YORK'S COLUMN AND STEPS [E5] (Waterloo Place, Trafalgar Square), like so many London statues, was erected to a now half-forgotten man—the second son of George III. Unfortunately, the internal staircase is no longer open to the public, so that the fine view to be had from the top is equally unavailable.

E

EARL'S COURT, Warwick Road, SW5 (Earl's Court Tube Station). A big clumsy building put up in the thirties as an exhibition and sports centre. Many exhibitions are staged there. It also has a swimming-pool and ice rink which is sometimes converted into a boxing arena.

EARLY AND LATE CLOSING. Usual shop hours are from 9 a.m. to 5.30 p.m. In the West End and City, shops close at one o'clock on Saturday until Monday morning. Local shops stay open on Saturday afternoons—often until seven or eight in the evening—and usually close instead on Thursday afternoons, sometimes on Wednesday. In Regent Street, Oxford Street and one or two other main West End shopping centres, there's a late opening on Thursdays until seven o'clock—a fairly recent and most sensible innovation.

EATING OUT. Eating out is by no means as dreary as many Londoners pretend. There's good food of all kinds to be had, and only meat is scarce. London still has the best fish and game in the world, and for generations the finest wines of France, Portugal and Spain have been shipped to this country.

The restaurants listed below break down into five main categories. The first, West End restaurants with dancing (and often cabaret) are, of course, pretty expensive, and you should reckon about 35/- per head for dinner, without wine. The second, West End restaurants without dancing, are less expensive, but (with the exception of those marked 'R' for reasonable) they will still set you back between £1 and 25/- for a meal. The third section—restaurants in Soho—vary quite a bit in price. At most of them, though, you can get a perfectly sound *table d'hôte* meal for

43

between 6/- and 12/6—it costs more, of course, if you start ordering specialities *à la carte*.

The fish (or sea food) restaurants are listed separately in a fourth section. They're a London feature which you should certainly try. In the last section come the awkward places which don't go into any of the other lists—just a few personal tips about out-of-the-way places, all-night restaurants, snack bars and so on.

It's as well to book a table in advance at practically any restaurant. This is a simple act of courtesy which will get you better service.

Two more points: don't be bullied by the wine waiter. The first three or four wines on the list are usually the best value for money; don't be frightened of ordering them because they are cheaper than the others.

Secondly, tipping: practically all restaurants operate the *tronc* system nowadays, whereby all tips are put into a central pool, so don't feel that you have to tip each waiter separately. I myself always add between 10 and 15 per cent to the bill, and leave it at that. If, of course, you feel that you've really been superbly looked after, leave a little more. Above all, tell the head waiter if you've had a good meal and thank him for it.

By and large, you will find that the restaurants of London are pretty good. There's still, perhaps, a little too much self-excusing being done on the grounds that life is difficult, and meat and butter and eggs and cream are hard to come by. The intelligent *restaurateur* prides himself on overcoming these difficulties. It's up to us—the people who keep them in business—to make sure that we get full value for our money. Every honest *restaurateur* welcomes this attitude.

WEST END RESTAURANTS WITH DANCING

Allegro, 16 Bury St. SW1
Quaglino's old Grill Room, now with a
vaguely West Indian atmosphere. Intimate
room with excellent service.   WHI 6767

Bagatelle, 1 Mayfair Place, W1
In the heart of Mayfair and conscious of it.   GRO 1268

Jack and Daphne Barker's, 99 Regent St. W1
Candlelit, intimate, Mediterranean décor.   REG 0362

The Berkeley Restaurant, 77 Piccadilly, W1
One of the smartest places before the war, and back on the map now, with support from debs.   REG 8282

Café de Paris, 3 Coventry St. W1
Has built up a glossy post-war reputation with top cabaret stars (like Noel Coward and Beatrice Lillie), and insists on evening dress on the main floor, although you need not dress if you have a table in the balcony.   GER 2036

Colony, Berkeley Square, W1
Long, large room, popular with overseas visitors and the rag trade.   MAY 1657

The Dorchester, Park Lane, W1
A large and splendid room, as you'd expect.   MAY 8888

Frascati, Oxford St. W1
Ornate and bustling; popular for parties; excellent wines; not pompous.   MUS 7417

Grosvenor House, Park Lane, W1
Fewer minks and magnates than the Dorchester, but still pretty grand.   GRO 6363

Hatchetts, 1 Dover St. W1
A charming downstairs room popular with people from the Shires.   REG 0217

Hungaria, 16 Lower Regent St. SW1
Warm and comfortable and bright, with good Hungarian cooking.   WHI 4222

Manetta's, Clarges St. W1
Rather bustling and noisy in the evenings; better for lunch.   GRO 2964

Mayfair Hotel, Berkeley St. W1
Good service, sound food. Popular with business men.   MAY 7777

Mirabelle, 56 Curzon St. W1
Very Mayfair, with quite good food. A
pleasant terrace for summer eating.　　　　GRO 1940

96 Piccadilly, W1
Good professional food and service.　　　　MAY 9661

Piccadilly Hotel, Piccadilly, W1
Popular with out-of-towners; solidly efficient.　REG 8000

Pigalle, 190 Piccadilly, W1
The floor show is lavish and long, and
prices are reasonable considering the scale
of the entertainment.　　　　　　　　　GRO 6423

Quaglino's, 16 Bury St. SW1
Service excellent; usually pleasantly quiet.　WHI 6767

Savoy Hotel Restaurant, Strand, WC2
Large room, popular with parties, and still
very much one of the top places.　　　　TEM 4343

Trocadero, Shaftesbury Avenue, W1
Business men's restaurant, with a remarkable
wine list.　　　　　　　　　　　　　GER 6920

The Washington, 6 Curzon St. W1
With a new bright post-war face; popular
with overseas visitors.　　　　　　　　GRO 6911

WEST END RESTAURANTS WITHOUT DANCING

L'Aperitif Grill, 102 Jermyn St. SW1
Quiet and pleasant. Better-known for lunch
than for dinner.　　　　　　　　　　WHI 1571

Baldwin's Hotel, 19 Dover St. W1
Excellent food, in an extremely exclusive
atmosphere.　　　　　　　　　　　　MAY 1757

Berkeley Buttery, Berkeley St. W1
Good for a quick cheap meal if you don't
stay too long at the bar. *R.*　　　　　REG 8282

Boulestin, 23 Southampton St. WC2
Sound food in placidly old-fashioned
surroundings.　　　　　　　　　　　TEM 7061

46

Brown's Hotel, Dover St. W1
Good food and service in quiet, traditional
atmosphere. REG 6020

Café Royal, 68 Regent St. W1
Both Grill Room and Brasserie still serve
excellent food and wine, even though the
latter has lost its beloved red plush seats. *R.* REG 8240

Caprice, Arlington St. SW1
Top stage and screen restaurant with excellent (and surprisingly reasonable) food. REG 5154

Carlton Grill, Haymarket, SW1
All that remains of the once great Carlton
(bombed during the war)—still keeps up the
best of the old tradition. WHI 7300

Claridges Restaurant, Brook St. W1
As good as one might expect. The
Causerie is airy and light, if you want a
quick meal. MAY 8860

Connaught Hotel, Carlos Place, W1
Excellent food and wine in exclusive
surroundings. GRO 2211

Le Coq d'Or, Stratton St. W1
Increasingly popular, as it deserves to be;
good cold table. MAY 3054

l'Ecu de France, 111 Jermyn St. SW1
Quietly and deliberately perfectionist in the
best French manner. Excellent wines. WHI 2837

Ivy, West St. W1
Still in the heart of theatreland, but quieter
than in its former celebrity-packed pre-
eminence. TEM 4751

Maison Basque, 11 Dover St. W1
A sound *cuisine* in a pleasantly peaceful
room. REG 2651

Martinez, 25 Swallow St. W1
Good Spanish food and wine, all very
reasonable. REG 5066

The Monico, Piccadilly Circus, W1
The place for a quickish, reasonable lunch or
dinner. *R.*   GER 7721

Overton's, 4 Victoria Buildings, SW1
A tiny room like a small dining-car where,
if you order in advance, you can have really
first-class food. (See also Sea Food.)   VIC 3774

Pastoria, St Martin's St. WC2
Sound hearty food; popular with stage
people.   WHI 8641

Ritz Hotel, Piccadilly, W1
Better known for lunch than for dinner, with
good service and food.   REG 8181

Rules, Maiden Lane, Strand, WC2
Pleasantly old fashioned; sound, reasonable
food. *R.*   TEM 5314

Savoy Grill, Strand, WC2
Famous *rendezvous* of everybody who's
anybody.   TEM 4343

Scott's, Coventry St. W1
Sound and Old-established. (See also Sea
Food.) *R.*   GER 7175

Simpson's, Strand, WC2
Next to Savoy Hotel. Still retains much of its
traditional (and world-famous) solidity and
Englishness. *R.*   TEM 7131

Verreys, 233 Regent St. W1
Cosy, pleasant, unpretentious restaurant.
R.   REG 4495

SOHO RESTAURANTS

Soho should be an adventure; it should be a matter of
finding out for yourself the sort of places you want to go
back to. Restaurants listed below are all reliable, and those
I have starred are my own personal favourites—they may
not be yours.

CHINESE

Choy's Chinese Restaurant, 45 Frith St. W1	GER 7109
Hong Kong Chinese, 58 Shaftesbury Ave. W1	GER 6847
**Ley On's*, 89–91 Wardour St. W1	GER 4657
Maxim's Chinese, 30 Wardour St. W1	GER 3724

FRENCH

Père Auguste, 37 Gerrard St. W1	GER 3878
La Belle Etoile, 17 Frith St. W1	GER 3603
Belle Meuniere, 5 Charlotte St. W1	MUS 4975
Café Bleu, 40 Old Compton St. W1	GER 1968
Escargot, 48 Greek St. W1	GER 4460
**L'Etoile*, 30 Charlotte St. W1	MUS 7189
Jardin des Gourmets, 5 Greek St. W1	GER 1816
Kettner's, 29 Romilly St. W1	GER 3437

GREEK

Akropolis, 25 Percy St. W1	MUS 2289
Crete, 19 Percy St. W1	MUS 4914
*White Tower, 1 Percy St. W1	MUS 2187

HUNGARIAN

Hungarian Csárda, 77 Dean St. W1	GER 1261

ITALIAN

Bertorelli's, 19 Charlotte St. W1	MUS 4174
Gennaro's, 44 Dean St. W1	GER 3950
Isola Bella, 15 Frith St. W1	GER 3911
*Quo Vadis, 26 Dean St. W1	GER 4809

SPANISH

Casa Pepe, 52 Dean St. W1	GER 3916
*Majorca, 66 Brewer St. W1	GER 6803

SEA FOOD

There's little to choose between the sea-food places listed below. All of them have their own individual *cachet*;

none are very cheap. My own favourites are *Cunningham's*, *Wheeler's* and *Wilton's*—but it's best to choose for yourself.

Bentley's Bar, 15 Swallow St. W1	REG 0431
Cunningham's, 51 Curzon St. W1	GRO 3141
Driver's, 46 Glasshouse St. W1	REG 4646
Mermaiden, Clarges St. W1	GRO 2964
Overton's, 4 Victoria Buildings, SW1	VIC 3774
Prunier's, 72 St James's St. SW1	REG 1373
Scott's, Coventry St. W1	GER 7175
Wheeler's, 19 Old Compton St. W1	GER 2706
Wilton's, 34 King St. St James's, SW1	WHI 8391

ROUND THE CORNER

There are reasonable restaurants round every corner in London. It's impossible to mention more than a few of them here, but just one or two personal tips are:

Canuto's, 88 Baker St. W1 (WEL 8146). Rather quiet, very reasonable.

De Hems, 11 Macclesfield St. W1 (GER 2494). Good English pub fare with excellent sea food.

Dickens and Jones, Regent St. W1. A quiet and spacious store restaurant with remarkably good food and service.

The Doctor's Café, 19 New Cavendish St. W1 (WEL 4251). Cooking which satisfies even the specialists of Harley Street. No licence.

Dover Street Buttery, Dover St. W1 (REG 6191). A relatively new, smart place, where you can have a good light meal in a hurry, with reasonable wines by the glass to wash it down.

D. H. Evans, Oxford St. W1. Perhaps the best value in store restaurants, with wine by the glass, and intelligent cooking.

The Gore Hotel, Queen's Gate, SW7 (KEN 3621). Reasonable food, and one of the best wine lists in London.

Holborn Restaurant, High Holborn, WC1 (HOL 8671). Gloomy but solid; magnificent wines.

The House of Hamburger, 1 Leicester St. WC2 (GER 4864). Specialises in fried fish and chips. Just the place for a meal after the cinema.

Layton's Wine Room, 2a Duke St. W1 (WEL 8808). A little place where you can eat and drink quietly and well.

Lyons Corner Houses (at Compton St. Marble Arch, and Tottenham Court Road) certainly deserve an accolade for the very high standards that they maintain at low prices, and for the excellent and reasonable wine they serve in their licensed restaurants.

Marks and Spencers, at their many stores all over London, serve the best value in sandwiches, to eat at the counter or to take away.

The Nag's Head, Covent Garden, WC2. If you're going to the opera or ballet, or just looking round Covent Garden, you can get an honest pub meal upstairs.

The Normandie, 163 Knightsbridge, SW7 (KEN 1400). A gay little place with satisfying food.

The Ox on the Roof, 353 King's Rd. SW3 (FLA 8947). An enterprising Chelsea restaurant where you buy your own bottle of wine across the road (or bring it with you) to drink with a sound cheap meal.

Selfridge's Snack Bar, Orchard St. W1. The right place for a late breakfast, or a salad while you're shopping.

Simpson's, Piccadilly, W1. This store has an excellent little downstairs coffee bar and restaurant.

York Minster, 49 Dean St. W1 (GER 2799). Known as the French pub; has an excellent upstairs dining-room.

If you want to eat something at a quarter-past four in the morning, there are a few places open all night. You can get the egg and chips type of meal at the *Minerva* (corner of George Street and Baker Street), or down in the East End at the Avenue Cafe in Aldgate Avenue (by Aldgate Tube station); a cup of coffee and a sandwich or sausage roll at the cabman's shelter at Hyde Park Corner; a sandwich at *George's Snack Bar* in Lovat Lane in the City. *Lyons Corner Houses* in the Strand and Coventry Street run all-night rooms.

EMBANKMENT, The, runs from Westminster Bridge to Blackfriars Bridge, on the north side of the river. Central London's only long riverside walk, it's a fascinating place for a sandwich lunch or an afternoon stroll on a summer's day. At night a place for idlers and lovers, with the lamps gleaming in the water below and the bridges traced faintly against the sky.

EMBASSIES. Addresses are given in the Telephone Directory under the names of the different countries.

EMPIRE STADIUM AND POOL (Tube to Wembley Park, or 18, 92, 83 bus). Built in 1923 for the British Empire Exhibition (the Pool was added later) this is where you'll go to see the Cup Final or the English–Scottish Soccer International or an ice-pantomime or a Speedway Test Match or the Amateur Boxing Association Championships or any one of half-a-hundred other things. Wembley (as it's more familiarly known) has regular greyhound-racing and ice-hockey. The outdoor Stadium holds 100,000, the Pool up to 11,000.

EMPRESS HALL (Tube to West Brompton, or 74, 30, 28, 31, 91 bus). A late Victorian building reconstructed as a stadium in the thirties, the Empress Hall now houses ice-shows, Brass Band contests, dancing championships, conferences and so on. Ice-hockey every Sunday with seating for 6,000.

EROS [D4] Piccadilly Circus, W1. That this inconsequential statue, balanced precariously on one foot, should stand in the centre of solid London, is a typical paradox of the English character. Anyway, we like it. It's our rallying point at times of merrymaking, as Buckingham Palace is in times of crisis. It exerts a hypnotic influence over young men on occasions like Boat Race or Election Night or New Year's Eve, compelling them to defy the (at those times) serried ranks of the Metropolitan Police, and climb over the fountains on to the statue itself. A popular meeting-place, it's perhaps London's most photographed landmark. Alas, nearly all the pre-war flower girls who sat at its foot have drifted away. Incidentally, it was originally de-signed by Sir Alfred Gilbert as a memorial to the seventh Lord Shaftesbury; and Eros's bow, in the act of burying a shaft, was intended, in an outrageously punning way, to point towards Shaftesbury Avenue.

EXERCISE. There are quite a few ways of getting exercise in London—you can row, ride, run; hit squash, tennis or golf balls; skate or swim; tramp the streets ; or travel on the Tube in the rush hour.

Listed below are details of a few of the places where you can take your exercise. GOLF, RIDING and SKATING are under separate headings later in the book.

Gymnastics. There are many gymnasia scattered about London, but to use them you usually have to be a member of a particular club. However, the Central Council of Physical Recreation hold classes which you can join. Several evenings a week, their gymnasia function in Chelsea and Paddington Street. Telephone MUS 0726 for details.

Rowing. Rowing boats can be hired (at about 2/6 per hour) on the Serpentine in Hyde Park, or on the lakes in Regent's Park and Battersea Park.

Running. You can use the running track in Regent's Park free of charge; Paddington Recreation Ground in Randolph Avenue, Maida Vale, will charge you 4d an hour.

Squash and Tennis. The Squash and Tennis School and Club at 55 Park Lane, WI (GRO 1797) welcomes visitors, and temporary membership can be arranged. There are coaches and facilities for squash, tennis, table tennis, badminton and golf practice.

Another good place for squash is at *Dolphin Square*, SW1 (134 bus stops outside the block of flats). 5/- per half-hour; 6/- for tuition. You can play squash more cheaply at *Paddington Sports and Bowling Club*, Castellain Road, W9 (CUN 1234), but it's advisable to take your own partner.

You can play tennis on excellent hard courts for 2/- an hour in the following London parks (just a few of the most central ones): Battersea Park, SW11 (MAC 1741); Kensington Memorial Recreation Ground, N. Kensington, W10 (LAD 2744); Lincoln's Inn Fields, WC1 (HOL 5194); Parliament Hill, Hampstead, N6 (GUL 4491); Ravenscourt Park, W6 (RIV 5503); Regent's Park, NW1 (WEL 8556); Waterlow Park, Highgate, N6 (ARC 2825). 'Phone and book a court in advance.

Most tennis clubs welcome visitors, and the following are a few of the most conveniently situated: Campden Hill, W8 (POP 2170); Holland Park, W14 (PAR 7157); Hurlingham, SW6 (REN 2662); Pembroke, W8 (WES 0481); West Kensington, W14 (FUL 3421); Highgate, N6 (MOU 4747). 'Phone and ask for details.

Swimming. Here are a few of the public swimming baths in London: Battersea, Latchmere Road, SW11; Chelsea, King's Road, SW3; Holborn, Endell Street, WC2 (open air) and Y.M.C.A., Gt Russell Street, WC1; Kensington, Lancaster Gate, W2; St Marylebone, Seymour Place, W1 and Regent Street Polytechnic, W1.

F

FASHION. The most exclusive *haute couture* houses are now organised into the Incorporated Society of London Fashion Designers—the Top Eleven, as they are called—and show their collections in the last week of January and the last week of July. You should write or telephone to the houses—preferably write—for an invitation to see a collection. These are, of course, the most expensive people. Suits range from £75 to £125; and evening gowns can cost up to £300 and more. Their names and specialities are:

Hardy Amies, 14 Savile Row, W1 (REG 0728). Suits and coats.

John Cavanagh, 26 Curzon St. W1 (GRO 1076). Sophisticated modernity.

Charles Creed, 31 Basil St. SW3 (KEN 3910). Tailor mades.

Norman Hartnell, 26 Bruton St. W1 (MAY 0992). Elaborate evening gowns. (The Court Dressmaker.)

Lachasse, 4 Farm St. W1 (GRO 2906). Tweeds.

Mattli, 12 Upper Grosvenor St. W1 (GRO 7821). Sophisticated lines.

Digby Morton, 54 Grosvenor Hill, W1 (MAY 7595). Tailored suits.

Peter Russell, 2 Carlos Place, W1 (GRO 1656). English classics.

Michael Sherard, 24 Connaught St. W2 (AMB 1302). Feminine line and colour.

Victor Stiebel, at Jacqmar, 16 Grosvenor St. W1 (MAY 6111). Cocktail and evening dresses.

Worth, 50 Grosvenor St. W1 (MAY 1903). Elaborate wedding or ball gowns.

FESTIVAL HALL [F5] SE1—erected on the Festival of Britain site in 1951, and London's only important public building since the war, it's an exhilarating example of modern architecture, and acoustically perfect. What's more, you can drink and dine there in an airy restaurant overlooking the river, a place to remember for summer evenings. Most of the year round, except for a summer ballet and dance season, the Hall is devoted to concerts. For details of programmes, see the Saturday editions of *The Times* or the *Daily Telegraph*. You can get to the South Bank by Tube to Waterloo, by foot across Waterloo Bridge or Hungerford Bridge, or, delightfully, by boat to Rodney Pier.

FLEET STREET [G4] (a continuation of the Strand to Ludgate Circus) takes its name from the old River Fleet, which is now covered over and runs into the Thames underneath Blackfriars Bridge. One of the world's magic names, it's the newspaper headquarters of an Empire. Along it, on either side, rise the offices of the great London daily and evening papers and of the news agencies. In it work the people who make news about the people who make news. To it belong half a hundred journalists' pubs, where many stories are born and many careers die. If you want to hear your favourite columnist telling another columnist what a good columnist he is, go and drink your lunch at *El Vino's* (where you can sit and drink a bottle of champagne cheaply and comfortably in the little back bar) or the *Clachan*, up the alley just next door, or the *Cock*, or the *Punch Tavern*, which are just four of the really good pubs that abound in this part of the world.

FLOWER SHOPS. London is sprinkled with flower-shops. Those listed below are my own personal selection.

Constance Spry, 64 South Audley St. W1	GRO 3324
Fresh Flowers, 47 Davies St. W1	MAY 3783
Moyses Stevens, Berkeley Square, W1 and	MAY 5211
146 Victoria St. SW1	VIC 5051
(For all-night delivery service, telephone VIC 5051)	
Selfridge's Flower Shop, Orchard St. W1	MAY 1234
West End Flower House, 405 Oxford St. W1	MAY 1215

FOG descends on London, darkening and deadening the streets for a few days, every November and December, but far less often than Hollywood would have you suppose. The London Particular, the old-fashioned pea-souper, is relatively rare nowadays, as more and more smoke-producing industry moves out to the suburbs. Nor does it choke communications as once it did. The Tube goes on running even when buses and taxis have gone off the streets. It's best to try and get home in daylight, though; otherwise you may find yourself getting lost only a few yards from your own front door.

The morning mists that wreathe themselves across the town in the autumn and winter months should not be confused with the real thing. They give a strange and softening loveliness to familiar buildings. You will find a stroll through the Park or up the Mall a revelation on a milky October morning.

FOOTBALL—and to ninety-nine out of a hundred Londoners the word means soccer, the original game which Londoners have been playing since at least the twelfth century. To the few, it means Rugby, a recent upstart, only a hundred or so years old, born at Rugby School. London's three most famous soccer teams—  the Arsenal, Tottenham Hotspur, and Chelsea—all have grounds within easy reach of the centre of town. The sporting pages of the papers give the fixtures and kick-off times every Saturday during the season, which runs from late August to late April. The final of the knock-out Cup competition is played at Wembley Stadium on the first Saturday in May. London clubs in the various divisions of the Football League are listed below with their nearest stations.

1st Division: Arsenal (Arsenal, Highbury Hill), Charlton (by train from Charing Cross to Charlton), Chelsea (Walham Green), Tottenham Hotspur (Manor House, thence trolleybus). 2nd Division: Brentford (Boston Manor, thence trolleybus), Fulham (Putney Bridge), West Ham (Upton Park). 3rd Division South: Crystal Palace (by train from Victoria or London Bridge to Selhurst), Leyton Orient (by train from Liverpool Street to Leyton), Millwall (New Cross), Queen's Park Rangers (Shepherd's Bush), Watford (Watford High Street).

In addition to these professional clubs, there is a considerably larger number of amateur clubs. The grounds are, of course, much smaller, and the standard of play lower. A few of the best-known are: Barnet, Finchley, Hendon and Walthamstow Avenue. The Amateur Cup Final takes place at Wembley on a late Saturday in April.

The headquarters of the Rugby game are at Twickenham, where various Internationals are played during the season. Perhaps the most hotly contested and violently supported match is the annual Oxford and Cambridge game, played in early December.

All Rugby Union clubs are amateur. Five of the best-known are:

Blackheath, Rectory Field (by train from Charing Cross or London Bridge to Blackheath, thence 54 or 75 bus). Harlequins, Fairfax Road (Teddington). Richmond, Old Deer Park (Richmond). Rosslyn Park, Kew Road (Richmond, thence 27 or 65 bus). Wasps, Eton Avenue (Sudbury Town).

G

GOLF. London is surrounded by golf clubs. Listed below are just a few of them. Average fees are 3/6 to 5/- for a round; 5/- to 10/- for the day. On week-ends and public holidays, of course, the fees are higher.

The best thing to do, as a visitor to London, if you are *not* being introduced by a member, is to write to the secretary of the club you fancy, and see whether he can give you temporary membership. He will also tell you how to get there.

Most clubs make a special effort to welcome visitors from overseas, and I have noted below, beside the clubs concerned, what you need to do.

Croydon, Surrey. Croham Hurst Club. No introduction needed.

Denham, Middlesex. Denham Club. Overseas visitors should have letter of introduction from British Travel and Holidays Association.

Ealing, Middlesex. Ealing Club, Perivale Lane, Greenford. No introduction needed.

Eltham, SE9. Eltham Warren Club, Bexley Road. Members of recognised overseas clubs welcome.

Enfield, Middlesex. Crews Hill Club, near Enfield. Overseas visitors should apply through British Travel and Holidays Association.

Hendon, NW4. Hendon Club, Holders Hill Rd. NW4. Overseas visitors received by Club Secretary.

Honor Oak, SE23. Honor Oak and Forest Hill Club, Honor Oak Park, SE23. Overseas visitors received by Club Secretary.

Pinner, Middlesex. Pinner Hill Club. Introduction required.

Purley, Surrey, Purley Downs Club, 106 Purley Downs Rd. No introduction needed.

Richmond, Surrey. Richmond Park Course, Putney, SW15. Introduction required.

Watford. West Hertfordshire Club, Cassiobury Park. No introduction needed.

Wimbledon, Surrey. Wimbledon Park Club, Home Park Rd. Overseas visitors welcome if members of a home club.

GREEN PARK [c & d 5] stretches itself elegantly on your left hand as you walk up Piccadilly towards Hyde Park Corner. A quiet and uncomplicated patch of green and trees, its other side is flanked by Constitution Hill, which runs down from Hyde Park Corner to St James's Park. On the far side of Constitution Hill lie Buckingham Palace Gardens.

GREYHOUND RACING has grown since its beginning here in the twenties to a great London sport. Meetings take place on weekday evenings, and on Saturday afternoons and evenings. For days and times—which vary at different tracks—see the London evening press or the *Greyhound Express*. At the White City you can dine in comfort and see the races at the same time. Harringay, Stamford Bridge and White City are only taxi rides from the West End.

TRACKS

Catford, Catford Bridge, SE6 (HIT 2261). Train to Catford Bridge.

Charlton, Woolwich Rd. SE7 (GRE 3301). Train from Charing Cross to Charlton.

Clapton, Millfields Road, E5 (AMH 3203). Tube to Bethnal Green or Manor House. Then bus or trolleybus.

Hackney Wick, Stratford, E15 (AMH 2516). Tube to Leyton, or No. 6 bus.

Harringay, Green Lanes, N4 (STA 3474). Tube to Manor House.

Hendon, North Circular Rd. NW2 (GLA 6257). Tube to Brent. Then 18 or 112 bus.

New Cross, Hornshay St. SE15 (NEW 0213). Tube to New Cross.

Park Royal, Abbey Rd. NW10 (ELG 4554). Tube to Park Royal.

Stamford Bridge, Fulham Rd. SW6 (FUL 4423). No. 14 bus.

Walthamstow, Chingford Rd. E4 (LAR 1428). No. 38 bus.

Wandsworth, Buckhold Rd. SW18 (VAN 4000). Tube to Clapham Common. Then 37 bus.

Wembley, Empire Stadium, Middlesex (WEM 1234). Tube to Wembley or Wembley Park.

West Ham, Custom House, E16 (ALB 2441). Tube to Plaistow. No. 699 trolleybus from there.

White City, Shepherd's Bush, W12 (SHE 5544). Tube to White City.

Wimbledon, Plough Lane, SW17 (WIM 5361). Tube to
Tooting Broadway. Then trolleybus.

GROSVENOR SQUARE [C4] W1. Until relatively recently, this was where noblemen had their tall town houses,
a glittering place during the Season, quiet for the rest of the
year. Nicknamed *Eisenhowerplatz* during the war, because
of the concentration of American troops around the U.S.
Embassy building there, recent years have seen no lessening
of American influence, and the Embassy continues to be a
dominating factor in the life of the Square, with Cadillacs
and Chevrolets parked nose to tail all the way round the
well-barbered lawns and flower-beds. Fittingly, the
ROOSEVELT MEMORIAL stands on the northern
side of the Square; an impressive standing statue, though
controversial at the time it was erected with money sub-
scribed by the public. The work of Sir Reid Dick, it was un-
veiled in 1948 by Mrs Roosevelt in the presence of the King
and Queen.

GUARDS, The. The Brigade of Guards, which provides
the Queen's Guard—those on sentry duty at Buckingham
Palace and St James's Palace—consists of five regiments:
the Grenadiers, the Coldstreams, the Scots, the Irish and
the Welsh. The person of the Sovereign is traditionally protected by the Household Cavalry; that is, the Life Guards
and the Royal Horse Guards (the Blues). The Household
Cavalry provides the mounted escort for the Queen on
State occasions and the guard which is mounted at the Horse
Guards building in Whitehall (see HORSE GUARDS).

On ceremonial occasions the foot regiments wear scarlet
uniforms with blue and white facings, and you can tell one
from another by their plumes and buttons. The Grenadiers
have white plumes and a single line of buttons down the
front of their tunics; the Coldstreams, red plumes and
buttons in pairs; the Irish, blue plumes and buttons in
fours. The Welsh have white plumes with a strip of green

and wear their buttons in fives. The Scots Guards have no plumes and their buttons are in threes.

Equally, you can tell the Life Guards from the Horse Guards by their ceremonial uniforms. The Life Guards have scarlet tunics, or in winter scarlet overcoats, white plumes and white lambskin saddles. The Royal Horse Guards wear blue tunics, blue coats, red plumes, and have black saddles.

On less formal occasions, you will see the tall figures of Guardsmen stepping smartly along in pairs around Hyde Park Corner and Marble Arch, in their walking-out uniforms. Officers walk out in mufti, which is as near a uniform as civilian clothes can get: bowler hat tilted forward above pink face and small moustache, Guards tie (diagonal red and blue stripes), blue suit, rolled umbrella and black shoes.

Often criticised as hidebound and old fashioned in times of peace, the Guards have continually performed prodigies in every war since Marlborough's time, and it's a happy regimental commander who knows that there's a Guards regiment on his flank.

GUILDHALL [H3] Moorgate, EC2 (Bank Tube Station).

 The Great Fire of 1666 destroyed the original fifteenth-century building, and today's exterior is largely eighteenth century. The great Blitz fire of 1940 destroyed the roof and some other parts, which have since been restored. The election of the Lord Mayor, and the Lord Mayor's Banquet, take place there every year. There's a small museum attached which holds some interesting historical relics. The Guildhall is open on weekdays from ten till five o'clock.

H

HAIRDRESSERS. London has always been better-known for men's hairdressing than for women's. The old-established barbers' shops of Mayfair are among the finest in the world; the three best known are:

Topper, 17 Old Bond St. W1	REG 3366
Truefitt & Hill, 23 Old Bond St. W1	REG 2961
Trumper, 9 Curzon St. W1	GRO 1850

Several men's stores also have excellent hairdressing shops, those at *Austin Reed's* and *Simpson's* being particularly well known. So have most large hotels, notably the *Ritz* and the *Savoy*.

A new generation of women's hairdressers has done something to even the balance. Among the best known are:

Antoine, 38 Dover St. W1	REG 2186
French, 4 Curzon Place, W1	GRO 3778
Raymond, 18 Grafton St. W1 and at	REG 7132
18 Albemarle St. W1	REG 6572
Riché, 14 Hay Hill, W1	REG 3368
Steiner, 66 Grosvenor St. W1	MAY 5245

Of course, most beauty salons have their own hairdressing departments, those at *Elizabeth Arden* and *Helena Rubenstein* being particularly well thought of. A number of department stores, too, have special hairdressing departments, those at *Harrods* and at *D. H. Evans* being among the best.

HAMPSTEAD HEATH. Real country to the Cockney, the Heath spreads its thickly-wooded greenness over six hundred rolling acres. The best way to get there is by Tube to Hampstead, turn right outside the station, and then walk up the winding hill with its little shops and tall houses to the Whitestone Pond, a paddling pool for children, on which flotillas of model yachts dip and scurry. From here you get a magnificent view down over the Vale of Health (where Leigh Hunt and others of the early Victorian great lived and worked) to the City, with the dome of St Paul's clearly visible on a fine day. It's here at Easter and Whitsun and the August Bank Holiday that the great Fair takes place, with its roundabouts, swings, steam-engine music, coconut shies and sideshows. Then the Heath is a noisy jumble of Londoners out for the day. On normal weekdays it's half-deserted. The best time to go, perhaps, is on a Sunday, when Hampstead is taking its constitutional there (a fair proportion in beards and corduroy trousers), and when the pubs like *The Spaniards* down by Ken Wood, and *Jack Straw's Castle* by the pond, are busy and companionable places.

HAMPTON COURT. Best known now, perhaps, for its pictures and maze in its grounds, Hampton Court was built by Cardinal Wolsey in 1514 (later additions by Inigo Jones and Sir Christopher Wren). He gave it to his friend, Henry VIII, all of whose six Queens lived there—consecutively, of course. Its lovely Thames-side gardens have made it the favourite summer palace of several monarchs. Elizabeth I spent much of her time there. Charles II honeymooned there. Less lucky, William III fell when his horse stumbled on a molehill, and was killed there. Now owned by the nation, the Palace is open on summer weekdays from 10 a.m. to 6 p.m. and on Sundays from 2 to 6, but the gardens stay open until 9. Delightful concerts of chamber music have been held in the Palace, and are worth looking out for. You can get there by Green Line bus—716, 717 or 718 from Hyde Park Corner, or train from Waterloo, or Tube to Wimbledon or Hammersmith, then trolleybus. Admission Monday to Friday 1/-, Saturday 6d. Sundays and Bank Holidays free.

HORSE GUARDS [E5]. Two mounted troopers of the Household Cavalry guard the entrance in Whitehall. Between the buildings, an archway leads to Horse Guards Parade, where the ceremony of Tropping the Colour takes place on the Queen's official birthday in June.

The ceremonial Mounting the Guard

takes place at the Horse Guards at eleven o'clock on week-days and ten o'clock on Sundays.

For details about the Household Cavalry, see the GUARDS.

HOSPITALS. See DOCTORS and DENTISTS.

HOTELS. London is teeming with hotels. Those listed below are simply a selection of the bestknown. Most of them are fairly expensive. There are, of course, large hotels at all railway termini, and great clusters of cheaper ones in Paddington, Victoria, South Kensington, Bayswater and Bloomsbury. (See also BED AND BREAKFAST.) Of those mentioned below, *Claridge's*, the *Connaught*, the *Ritz* and *Brown's* are perhaps the most exclusive; the *Savoy* and the *Dorchester* the minkiest.

Athenaeum Court, 116 Piccadilly, W1 (Suites)	GRO 3464
Basil Street Hotel, Knightsbridge, SW1	SLO 3411
Berkeley Hotel, 77 Piccadilly, W1	REG 8282
Brown's Hotel, Dover St. W1	REG 6020
Claridge's Hotel, Brook St. W1	MAY 8860
Connaught Hotel, Carlos Square, W1	GRO 2211
Cumberland Hotel, Marble Arch, W1	AMB 1234
Dorchester Hotel, Park Lane, W1	MAY 8888
Durrant's Hotel, George St. Manchester Square, W1	WEL 8131
Grosvenor House, Park Lane, W1	GRO 6363
Hyde Park Hotel, Knightsbridge, SW1	SLO 4567
Imperial Hotel, Russell Square, WC1	TER 3655
Mayfair Hotel, Berkeley St. W1	MAY 7777
Meurice Hotel, Bury St. W1	WHI 6767
Mount Royal Hotel, Marble Arch, W1	MAY 8040
Normandie Hotel, 163 Knightsbridge, SW1	KEN 1400

Park Lane Hotel, Piccadilly, W1	GRO 6321
Piccadilly Hotel, Piccadilly, W1	REG 8000
Regent Palace Hotel, Glasshouse St. W1	REG 7000
Ritz Hotel, Piccadilly, W1	REG 8181
Royal Court Hotel, Sloane Square, SW1	SLO 9191
Russell Hotel, Russell Square, WC1	TER 6470
Saint Ermin's Hotel, Caxton St. SW1	WHI 3176
Saint James's Court, Buckingham Gate, SW1	
(Suites)	VIC 2360
Savoy Hotel, Strand, WC2	TEM 4343
Stafford Hotel, St James's Place, SW1	REG 0111
Strand Palace Hotel, Strand, WC2	TEM 8080
Waldorf Hotel, Aldwych, WC2	TEM 2400
Washington Hotel, Curzon St. W1	GRO 6911

HOUSE AGENTS. There's still a housing shortage in London. Flats can be found, but they tend to be expensive by pre-war standards. You'll find the British Travel and Holidays Association helpful if you are an overseas visitor. Various embassies, too, have special departments to help their nationals find houses. Still the most sensible thing to do is to go to a reputable house agent. A few of them are listed below. Above all, don't go to an obviously fly-by-night establishment, whatever stories you hear about the wonders they can perform. Among the most reliable West End house agents are:

Hampton & Sons, 6 Arlington St. SW1	REG 8222
Knight, Frank & Rutley, 20 Hanover Square, W1	MAY 3771
Nicholas, 4 Albany Court Yard, Piccadilly, W1	REG 1184
Tressidder & Co., 77 South Audley St. W1	GRO 2861
George Trollope & Sons, 25 Mount St. W1	GRO 1553
Winkworth & Co., 48 Curzon St. W1	GRO 3121
John D. Wood & Co., 23 Berkeley Square, W1	MAY 6341

You will also find reliable local house agents in whatever district of London you're living. You should be able to get their addresses from your nearest library or post office.

HOUSES OF PARLIAMENT [E5 & 6]. Mistaken by many visitors for a truly historic building, the present Houses of Parliament, although they stand on the ancient site of the Palace of Westminster, were built in 1840, after a fire had almost entirely destroyed the old Palace some six years before.

The House of Commons is even more recent. It was destroyed by a bomb during World War II, and the Commons returned to it only in 1951 after it had been completely rebuilt.

Parliamentary government, perhaps Britain's best-known (and most valuable) contribution to the world, developed gradually. At first, Parliament was little more than an occasional assembly of feudal chieftains called together to help the king when he wanted money or men. It developed over the years into the House of Lords, the hereditary body, and the House of Commons (representatives of the people first met in 1264), the elected body.

Over the centuries, as power shifted slowly from the barons to the burghers, the Commons became more and more influential.

Parliament today consists of the Queen, the House of Lords and the House of Commons. Nearly all legislation is initiated in the Commons; it is then either revised by the Lords or returned by them to the Commons for revision, and, after final approval by both Houses, is ratified by the Queen.

You can see over the Houses of Parliament on Saturdays between 10 a.m. and 3.30 p.m. Try, if you can, to spare the time to listen to a debate. You can get into the Public Gallery after 4.15 p.m. on weekdays (11.30 a.m. on Fridays) by applying to the Admission Order Office, St Stephen's Hall, Westminster, or by getting a Member of Parliament (very busy men these days) to get you an order himself. (See also BIG BEN and WESTMINSTER HALL.)

HYDE PARK [A, B, C, 4 & 5]. London's best-loved park was characteristically appropriated from the monks of Westminster Abbey (who had held it as the Manor of Hyde since the Norman Conquest) by Henry VIII, who wanted a handy hunting enclosure.

So it remained until Charles I began to smarten it up with a circular drive and a racecourse, although in the wilder parts deer were still hunted up to the middle of the eighteenth century.

The haunt of footpads and highwaymen and a favourite duelling ground, it only turned respectable in 1851, when the Great Exhibition was held there. Sir Joseph Paxton's famous exhibition building (re-erected at Sydenham as the Crystal Palace, and later burnt down) covered twenty acres between Knightsbridge and Rotten Row. The only problem about the building, you may have heard, was the sparrows; and one of the Duke of Wellington's last services to his Sovereign (who was perturbed by the birds' habits) was to offer a typically tight-lipped solution: 'Sparrow-hawks, Ma'am'.

Today, Hyde Park is London's most important green lung. You can row or swim at the Serpentine; you can ride in Rotten Row; at Speakers' Corner (see MARBLE ARCH), you can get up and speak about the evils of everything, or heckle everyone who's speaking; you have enough room to take a decent walk; or you can, as hundreds of thousands of Londoners do on any summer day, just stretch out and go to sleep on the grass.

Parisians boast about the Bois de Boulogne. But some of Hyde Park's vistas—the view across the grass through the trees from Knightsbridge Barracks on a hazy spring morning, for example—can't be equalled anywhere. Or just stand on the bridge across the Serpentine, and look around you; and I know you'll agree with me.

I

INNS OF COURT, The, form four pools of peace on either side of the Strand just by the Royal Courts of Justice [F3 & 4].

In order to practise as a barrister, you must be a member of one of the Inns, which contain the barristers' chambers, as their consulting rooms are called.

On the south side of the Strand, where it becomes Fleet Street, are the Inner Temple and Middle Temple [F & G4]. These two Inns derive their names from their association with the Knights Templar, which dates from 1160.

The Temple is still allowed to assess its own rates, and although it is just inside the City boundaries (marked by Temple Bar in the Strand) it's the only place in the City which the Lord Mayor cannot enter in state. Lawyers, in their hard-headed way, have always refused to admit his jurisdiction. Although the original Temple (which gave the place its name) was destroyed during the war, the Temple Church has survived both the Great Fire of 1666 and the blitz. Entrance to the Temple is through a venerable iron-studded oak door, and once past it, as you wander down the gentle slope towards the river through quiet grey court-yards, you're in another world.

On the other side of the street, behind the Law Courts, lies Lincoln's Inn [F3] and beyond Holborn lies Gray's Inn [F3], both taking their names from legal celebrities of the thirteenth century, Lord Walter de Grey, a famous Lord Chancellor, and the Earl of Lincoln, a judge.

As you stroll through them, it seems almost inconceivable that so little should have changed. The sound of buses and cars, a ship hooting down on the Thames, the shout of a paper-seller, a clock chiming distantly—the whole fibre of London's noise comes only faintly to you, muted and muffled by the centuries.

J

JOHNSON'S LONDON. Many of the places where one  of the greatest of Londoners lived and worked have disappeared with the cobbled streets and sedan chairs and coffee shops. But enough remain to serve as an informal memorial to him, besides the bust in Poets' Corner at Westminster Abbey, the statues in St Paul's and in St Clement Dane's in the Strand, his own parish church.

The Cheshire Cheese, [G3] his favourite tavern, still stands in Fleet Street, and the talk is still writers' talk. Johnson's Court, and Johnson's Buildings in the Temple, commemorate houses that he lived in, and Gough Square [G3] off Fleet Street, where he lived for ten prolific years from 1748, producing *The Rambler* and the great Dictionary, is still very much as it was then. His house, Number 17, has been preserved as a memorial, poorly furnished as it would have been in his time—for those were lean years for him. You can see there the large attic in which Johnson and his six scribes worked on the Dictionary.

'When a man is tired of London, he is tired of life; for there is in London all that life can afford', said the Doctor. And nearly two hundred years ago he gave some advice on how to see it which still stands: 'Sir, if you wish to have a just notion of the magnitude of this city, you must not be satisfied with seeing its great streets and squares, but must survey the innumerable little lanes and courts. It is not in the showy evolutions of buildings, but in the multiplicity of human habitations which are crowded together, that the wonderful immensity of London consists'.

K

KEATS' HOUSE, Wentworth Place, Keats' Grove, NW3 (Tube to Belsize Park, or No. 24 bus). Preserved as a memorial to the poet. Even the surroundings have changed very little from his day to ours.

KENSINGTON—the *Royal* Borough of Kensington, as its residents like to emphasise in a quiet and well-bred way—is still London's quietest and best-bred residential quarter. Spreading west from Knightsbridge and Belgravia, Kensington is an area of large, gently decaying houses, leafy squares and tree-lined terraces. While much of Victorian solidity remains, twilight shabbiness  is falling over the Royal Borough. The large clumsy houses are carved unfeelingly into one-room flatlets; the nameplates of cheap hotels spread through the streets like a rash.

A famous shopping centre, with several great stores clustered together in Kensington High Street (see SHOPPING), the Borough also embraces Kensington Church Street, which holds more antique shops than any other London street of its length.

Here, too, is Kensington Palace, which became a royal palace when William III bought it from the Earl of Nottingham. Christopher Wren enlarged it; Grinling Gibbons carved in it. It was here that the eighteen-year-old Victoria was called from her bed in the early hours of the morning by the insistent knocking of the Archbishop of Canterbury and the Lord Chamberlain, who had come to tell her that she was Queen. You can see the state apartments on Saturday and Sunday afternoons. Admission 6d. The Palace also houses the London Museum (see MUSEUMS).

Kensington Gardens, an extension of Hyde Park towards the Palace, are quiet and graceful. A part is specially laid out for children, and the Round Pond is the Cowes of the model yacht world. The Peter Pan statue and the Elfin Oak carved with animals and gnomes, which is in the children's playground, are both favourite attractions.

KEW. At Kew are the largest botanical gardens in the world, containing almost every known variety of shrub, tree and flower. In the great conservatory, plants flower all the year round; and there are fern houses, the cactus house, the Alpine house, the winter garden, the palm house and the succulent house. Thousands of Londoners, however, pay little attention to the more esoteric plants; they go to Kew to look at the flowers, to sleep on the grass, and listen to the birds. Their example is well worth following, particularly in spring and early summer.

All this began with Princess Augusta, the mother of George III, who started an Exotic Garden there in 1760. Kew Palace (or the Dutch House, as it's often called) dates from that time, and contains a delightful collection of pictures and furniture owned by George III and his family.

The gardens are open every day from ten o'clock until sunset, the glasshouses from 1 to 5 p.m. Admission is 3d. You get there by a 27 bus, or by Tube, District Line to Kew.

L

LAMBETH, SE1, is the home both of the cheerful Cockney *Lambeth Walk* of pre-war days, and LAMBETH PALACE [F6] (in Lambeth Road) which has been the official London residence of the Archbishop of Canterbury for the last seven hundred years.

In the heart of Cockneydom, it's an ideal place to meet the real Londoner, to have a glass of beer with him in a pub, or a cuppa and a cheese roll in a café. The Archbishop of Canterbury is more difficult to meet.

LAW COURTS [F3 & 4] Fleet Street, EC4. This large, Victorian Gothic building (built in 1873) stretches from Fleet

Street to Carey Street. Known officially as the Royal Courts of Justice, it houses nineteen courts, serving the Queen's Bench, the Chancery, Probate, and Divorce and Admiralty Divisions and the Court of Appeal.

You can go into the public galleries whenever you want to, and the ushers will usually tell you where the most interesting case is on, depending on your taste. When you become tired of legalities, you can go and have a drink in the Crypt Bar with barristers (the happy-looking ones) and their clients (the worried-looking ones).

LEICESTER SQUARE [E4]. The heart of London's cinema district, it lies between Piccadilly Circus and Charing Cross Road.

It was built shortly after the Restoration, when houses were put up on three sides of a field facing Leicester House, built in 1630 by the second Earl of Leicester. Among famous Londoners who once lived here were Newton, Hogarth and Reynolds, of whom there are busts in the central garden. Gradually the Square became more shabby and more disreputable, until in 1874 the present gardens were laid out. They are now peopled by lovers, sleepy old men with newspapers and Shakespeare, whose statue eyes the Empire cinema (with a mild surmise) from the centre of the gardens.

LIBRARIES.

PUBLIC LIBRARIES

There are free public libraries in every borough. If you are a visitor, you must find two ratepayers to vouch for you before you can borrow books. But you may use the reading-rooms anyway.

MUSEUM LIBRARIES

The museums listed below also have reference libraries which may be used free on application.

British Museum Reading-Room, Bloomsbury. (You must make written application.)

County Hall, Westminster. (Local government and topography.)

Geological Museum, South Kensington.

Patent Office, Chancery Lane. (Technical and scientific.)

Public Record Museum, Chancery Lane. (Historical.)

Science Museum, South Kensington.

Victoria and Albert Museum, South Kensington. (The arts.)

PRIVATE SUBSCRIPTION LIBRARIES

These exist in all areas of London, and the charges vary. The best known are:

Army and Navy Stores Library, 105 Victoria St. SW1.

Boots Libraries. (Branches at most Boots shops.)

Harrods Library, Brompton Rd. SW1.

London Library, 14 St James's Square, SW1. (Founded by Thomas Carlyle in 1841. Incorporated by Royal Charter in 1933. Independent and non-profit-making, being financed only by subscriptions and bequests. Library policy controlled by Committee of persons from all walks of public life. 750,000 volumes, and 7,000 books are added every year. New members only admitted on recommendation of an established member. Subscription 6 guineas annually. Members are allowed ten books at a time—fifteen if country members. In exceptional cases visitors may use the Reading-Room on payment of a monthly subscription of 10/6. Large reading-room with reference books and periodicals.)

W. H. Smith & Son, Ltd. (Branches at most W. H. Smith shops.)

Times Book Club, 42 Wigmore St. W1.

LICENSING HOURS. The British licensing hours are no more understandable in London than they are anywhere else in the country. Licensing laws are a jumble of inconsistencies arising out of the Defence of the Realm Act of the first World War, which has never been adequately revised. Opening and closing times of pubs vary little, but the small variations can be annoying. If you know how to do it, you can, of course, drink all round the clock in London: start off at Covent Garden or Billingsgate before dawn, when you're thrown out of there, go to an ordinary pub, then to an afternoon drinking club (most of them operate from 3 to 11 p.m.) when the pubs shut; go on to a night club when you're thrown out of there; and then, if you can still take it, start all over again. You'll find no legal way of getting a drink after half-past two in the morning, but in some places coffee cups have a habit of getting filled with things other than coffee.

Licensing hours of pubs vary according to districts, and are listed below.

> *Mayfair, Westminster, Victoria, Holborn:*
> Weekdays—11.30–3: 5.30–11
> Sundays 12.30–2.30: 7–10
>
> *Chelsea, Kensington, Fulham, Hammersmith:*
> Weekdays—11–3: 5.30–10.30
> Sundays 12–2: 7–10
>
> *Paddington:*
> Weekdays—same as Mayfair
> Sundays—12–2: 7–10
>
> *City:*
> Weekdays—11.30–3: 5–10.30
> Sundays—same as Mayfair

LINCOLN, ABRAHAM [E5] Parliament Square. The greatest American, as many of us think him, stands dreaming close by the Houses of Parliament. The statue is a replica of the St Gauden one which stands in Lincoln Park, Chicago. Offered us by America in 1914, to commemorate a hundred years of peace between the English-speaking peoples, it was put up in 1920.

LLOYD'S [J4] Leadenhall Street, EC3. The most famous insurance house in the world takes its name from an old coffee-house where, in seventeenth-century Lombard Street, shipowners met to discuss business. The main chamber is still called the Room, the uniformed attendants are known as waiters, and the desks arranged just like the seats in the vanished coffee-house.

Not strictly an insurance company, Lloyd's consists of a group of individual underwriters, each making himself responsible for part of the risk, and accepting a part-premium in return. The famous Lutine Bell (saved from the wreck of a French man-o'-war in the eighteenth century) makes underwriters blench when it is rung once—to announce disaster—and smile when it is rung twice—for good news.

LONDON COUNTY COUNCIL. See COUNTY HALL.

LONDON STONE [H4]. In the wall of St Swithin's Church, Cannon Street, near the station, is the London Stone. In Roman Londinium, set in the wall of the Forum, it marked the central point of the City, from which all distances were measured on the Roman roads which arrowed to the four corners of the country. The Forum stood, by the way, where Leadenhall Market now stands, and many remains have been found in the area. Excavation in the district is still going on.

LORD MAYOR, The. London has had a Mayor since the twelfth century, when King John granted its citizens the right to elect one annually. He has been referred to as Lord Mayor since 1283, though he's not a peer—it's just a courtesy title. His election by the Sheriffs and Aldermen of the City of London takes place every year in the Guildhall, which is strewn for the ceremony with sweet smelling herbs —a reminder of the days when London literally stank.

Once elected, the new Lord Mayor drives in state through

the City. This drive is the **LORD MAYOR'S SHOW,** and has been taking place since the thirteenth century, when the election had to be confirmed by the King at the Palace of Westminster. The Lord Mayor rides through the City streets in a gilded coach which, while being splendid to look at, and one of the most venerable vehicles in use, has neither springs nor brakes. He goes from Guildhall to the Royal Courts of Justice by way of Gresham Street, Threadneedle Street, Mansion House Street, Poultry, Cheapside, Ludgate Hill and Fleet Street, and then back to the Mansion House by way of Victoria Embankment and Queen Victoria Street. The Show takes place on 9th November each year (except when it falls on a Sunday) and is a traditional treat for London's children.

The Lord Mayor (who receives a salary of £12,500 for his year's work, but has so many commitments that only a rich man can accept the office) has his official residence in the **MANSION HOUSE** [H4] near the Bank of England, which was built in 1739. It's the last of the City's great houses. Its Banqueting Hall and Ballroom, known as the Egyptian Hall, is a vast room which contains some of the sculpture designed for the Great Exhibition of 1851.

Permission can usually be obtained to see the Mansion House by writing to the Lord Mayor's secretary.

LORD'S [A1] St John's Wood Road, NW8. The headquarters of cricket, home of the Marylebone Cricket Club—the arbiters of the game—and the Middlesex County Cricket Club, is the loveliest place in the world in which to watch the loveliest of all games.

The name of the ground has nothing to do with the peerage. It was a Mr Lord who first developed the ground. Several moves were made (but each time the original turf was shifted) before the present ground in St John's Wood became the home of the Marylebone

77

Club a hundred years or so ago. Take a 2, 13 or 74 bus, or the Tube to St John's Wood. Go there on a sunny summer afternoon after lunch. You can have a drink at the Tavern while you watch the cricket with hundreds of Londoners, who were saying in the office half an hour ago that they really thought they had better go and see a chap called Smith down in the City, and wouldn't be back for the rest of the day.

LOST PROPERTY OFFICES. If you lose something, whether *in a taxi, a public park or the street*, go either to the nearest police station or the Lost Property Office at 109 Lambeth Road, SE1. Open 10 a.m. to 4 p.m. *No enquiries answered on the telephone.*

In main-line trains or stations, enquire at the station of arrival or at the Head Office of the Railway Region concerned.

In buses, Tubes or Tube stations, go to the Lost Property Office next to Baker Street Station (ABB 1234). Open Monday to Friday: 10 a.m. to 6 p.m. Saturday: 10 a.m. to 1 p.m. *No enquiries answered on the telephone.*

If you want to buy an umbrella, a raincoat or a suitcase cheap, these sorts of things, lonely and unclaimed, are on sale at Lost Property Sales Offices at:

103 New Oxford St. WC1
239 Oxford St. W1
87 Regent St. W1
150 Strand, WC2
3 Hudson Place (adjoining Victoria Station), SW1
96a Victoria St. SW1

'LOVELY SWEET VIOLETS!' was the famous cry —one of London's last-remaining street cries—of the septuagenarian flower girls of Piccadilly Circus. You still hear it sometimes in the purlieus of Haymarket and Coventry Street. The violets are dearer now; but they're still as sweet.

M

MANSION HOUSE. See LORD MAYOR.

MARBLE ARCH [B4] W1. The Marble Arch itself was
originally designed by John Nash
to form an entrance to Buckingham
Palace, but alas, when it was put up,
they found that, by some slight
oversight, they had made it too
narrow for the State Coach to get
through. It was therefore removed,

to the accompaniment of snickers, to its present site as a
formal entrance to Hyde Park. The need for wider streets
forced the Park back in 1908, and now it is simply something
round which the victorious buses and taxis swoop with
grinding gears. It was near here that Tyburn Tree—London's last public gallows—stood until the end of the
eighteenth century. This is the popular end of the Park,
where the crowds are thickest and the grass is thinnest, and
here too, at SPEAKERS' CORNER, day in, day out,
but most vociferous on summer Sunday evenings, are the
orators and the hymn-singers, the crackpots and the
Coloured People's League, the reciters of Dangerous Dan
McGrew and the down-with-everything boys, all of them
surrounded by their mixed crowd of acolytes and hecklers.
Some of them are paid street-corner speakers of political
parties; some are missionary workers from any one of a
hundred churches; some are just speaking because they
like speaking; all of them—from the little man of sixty-five
with the wispy moustache, who's telling seven people that
the whole of history is written in the Great Pyramids and
who is too modest even to have a soap-box to stand on, to
the violently gesticulating Left-Wing speaker surrounded by
a crowd of a thousand or more, who are heckling him fiercely
as he attacks British policy in Africa—all of them have

something to say. Provided they don't attack the Royal Family (Buckingham Palace is just over there behind the trees in the sunset), or cause a riot, they can say anything they like. And the odd policeman standing about, trying hard to look as though he's not interested in what the speaker's saying, is, you will notice, more inclined to ask over-eager hecklers who are spoiling the fun to move on than to ask the speaker to tone down what he's saying.

MARKETS. Smithfield (meat), Covent Garden (fruit

and vegetables), Billingsgate (fish), and, on a Sunday morning, Petticoat Lane (for almost everything), are all dealt with under their own headings. Apart from these four, there are smaller street markets scattered all over London. In Soho's Berwick Street and the side turnings off it, there's an excellent all-the-week-round market, which is particularly busy on Saturday mornings. Also on weekdays, Fridays and Saturdays being the best times, you might have a look at Lambeth market (which will prove to you that there actually is a street called Lambeth Walk), or the Portobello Road in North Kensington, where you can buy a million things as well as the furniture and antiques that it's better-known for. Another one to have a look at is the Borough Market, the poor man's Covent Garden, in the shadow of Southwark Cathedral. Leadenhall Market, for poultry and fish wholesalers, stands on the site of the old Roman Forum.

MARLBOROUGH HOUSE [D5] Pall Mall, SW1. Famous latterly as the residence of Queen Mary, it was originally built by Wren for the first Duke of Marlborough, ancestor of Winston Churchill.

MAYFAIR. London s most fashionable quarter, as the rents of the flats and the people on the streets will demonstrate, can be taken as the square formed by Park Lane, Piccadilly, Bond Street and Oxford Street. It takes its name from a rowdy eighteenth-century version of Hampstead Heath on Bank Holiday, which erupted in the green fields of those days every May.

A few great houses which were built there soon won to themselves the squares and streets that we know today, but which are now full of luxury hotels, restaurants and smart shops. As large town houses become increasingly impracticable, so further changes are taking place. Business or Government offices have taken control of the main squares and streets, and it is only in the side turnings and in the mews that the residential life of the district flourishes. For all this, Mayfair has lost little of its *cachet*, and the name still has magic. To see the best of Mayfair, start off at Marble Arch, walk along Park Lane to Upper Grosvenor Street, down here and into Grosvenor Square, then into the continuation of Grosvenor Street on the other side; then take the first on the right, which is Davies Street, walk round three sides of Berkeley Square and up Charles Street, turning left along Queen Street to Curzon Street, then across the road, through the alleys into Shepherd Market, and so out into Piccadilly facing Green Park. Take your time as you stroll along; you'll see a lazy and lovely world that's disappearing.

MESSENGERS. Hand deliveries of parcels or letters anywhere in London are dealt with by the following people. Remember that they do not usually take orders after 5 p.m.

Theatre Tickets & Messengers Ltd. 191
Piccadilly, W1   REG 1026

and branches at:

    4 Charing Cross, SW1   WHI 7221
    1 Air St. W1   REG 5255
    100 St Martin's Lane, WC2   TEM 1023

109 Southampton Row, WC1   MUS 0627
193 Victoria St. SW1   VIC 5019
British Legion Employment Dept. 26 Eccleston Square, SW1   VIC 7661

MEWS. You'll find a surprising number of Londoners living in mews flats or houses. Much sought after now, because they're small, compact, and easy to heat and clean, these were originally the homes of coachmen and ostlers of the great houses, and in the present garages—many of them converted into ground-floor living-rooms—were kept the horses and coaches. Why mews? Because in the long story of London, even the coachmen were only a chapter—before that, it was in these side turnings that the hawks and falcons of earlier dwellers in earlier great houses were caged, or mewed.

MINT, The Royal [K4] Tower Hill, EC1 (Tube to Tower Hill). Once English kings had finally established a monopoly in the minting of coins (this took a good few hundred years), they had the job done at the Tower of London until, in 1810, the Royal Mint was erected just opposite. Here you can see every British coin being made, from a farthing to a Coronation crown, as well as the coins of many other countries and medals and insignia of all kinds. Try to fit in a visit if you can (write to the Controller for admission)—it's a fascinating place. And it's remarkable how the men who work there still manage to raise a laugh if you ask them, just as everyone else does and has since 1810, if they can let you have some samples.

MONUMENT, The [J4] (close to Monument Tube Station). Designed by Wren to commemorate the Great Fire of 1666, the Doric column is topped by a spiked football which is supposed to look like a ball of fire. How could Wren of all people have spoilt a graceful column in this way? There's a reason for it. You see, he made the column exactly two hundred and two feet high, because that was the precise distance to the site from the origin of the Fire in Pudding Lane. And all along, being a scientific man in a scientific age, he had intended it to work as a fixed telescope. Unfortunately Wren's grasp of architecture was sounder than his grasp of optics: two hundred and two feet was discovered to be an insufficient focal length—hence no telescope—and hence the spiked after-thought.

There's a fine view from the top, but three hundred and eleven steps to climb before you get there. Don't bother if you're feeling suicidal; the gallery is now caged in. Open 9 a.m. to 5 p.m. (4 p.m. on Sundays). Admission 3d.

MOUNT PLEASANT [G2] Rosebery Avenue, EC1. Write to the Divisional Controller's Office, Mount Pleasant, if you want to have a look at the headquarters of the Post Office where all the letters are sorted. A terrifyingly efficient giant of a building, the best time to see it is around six o'clock in the evening. Don't miss the automatic railway, Heartbreak Corner (in the Parcels Department) or Blind Letter Corner.

MUSEUMS.

BRITISH MUSEUM, Great Russell Street, WC1. (Tube to Russell Square or Tottenham Court Road.) With its Egyptian, Greek and Roman antiquities, its rare books and its fabulous collections, this is a must for any visitor. Open weekdays, including Bank  Holidays, 10 a.m. to 5 p.m. Sundays 2.30 to 6 p.m. Admission free.

GEFFRYE MUSEUM, Kingsland Road, E2. (Tube to Liverpool Street or Old Street, or No. 22 bus.) Social history from Elizabethan times to today. Open Tuesday–Friday

10 a.m. to 9 p.m. Saturdays 10 a.m. to 5 p.m. Sundays 2 to 5 p.m. Closed Mondays. Admission free.

GEOLOGICAL MUSEUM, Exhibition Road, SW7. (Tube to South Kensington.) Open weekdays, including Bank Holidays, 10 a.m. to 6 p.m. Sundays 2.30 to 6 p.m. Admission free.

HOME OFFICE INDUSTRIAL MUSEUM, 97 Horseferry Road, SW1. (Tube to St. James's Park.) Safety appliances, etc. Open weekdays 10 a.m. to 4 p.m. Closed Sundays. Admission free.

IMPERIAL INSTITUTE, Exhibition Road, SW7. (Tube to South Kensington.) Resources of the Commonwealth. Open weekdays 10 a.m. to 4.30 p.m. Closed Sundays. Empire films are shown in the Institute Cinema, at 3.30 p.m. on weekdays, and 2.30 and 3.30 p.m. on Saturdays. Admission free.

IMPERIAL WAR MUSEUM, Lambeth Road, SE1. (No. 10 bus from Victoria.) Open weekdays, including Bank Holidays, 10 a.m. to 6 p.m. Sundays 2 to 6 p.m. Admission free.

KENWOOD, IVEAGH BEQUEST, Hampstead Heath. (Tube to Golders Green or Archway, thence No. 210 bus.) Preserved as an eighteenth-century home, with fine collections of china, pictures and furniture. Open weekdays 10 a.m. to 6 p.m. Sundays 2 to 6 p.m. Admission free, except Wednesdays and Fridays—1/-. Restaurant attached, in the converted stables.

LONDON MUSEUM, Kensington Palace, Kensington Gardens, W8. (Nos. 9, 12 or 88 buses.) Best place to learn the history of London, with excellent early plans and models of the city. Open 10 a.m. to 4 p.m. Sundays 2 to 4 p.m. (6 p.m. in summer). Admission free.

NATIONAL MARITIME MUSEUM, Greenwich. (Train from Charing Cross to Greenwich or by river bus.) Open 10 a.m. to 6 p.m. Sundays 2.30 to 6 p.m. Admission free.

NATURAL HISTORY MUSEUM, Cromwell Road, SW7. (Tube to South Kensington.) Open weekdays, including

Bank Holidays, 10 a.m. to 6 p.m. Sundays 2.30 to 6 p.m. Admission free.

PUBLIC RECORD OFFICE MUSEUM, Chancery Lane, WC2. (Tube to Chancery Lane.) State papers and records. Open Monday to Friday 1 to 4 p.m. Closed Saturday and Sunday. Admission free.

ROYAL UNITED SERVICES MUSEUM, Whitehall, SW1. (Tube to Trafalgar Square, or Nos. 3, 12 or 88 buses.) Uniforms, weapons and equipment of armed forces past and present. Open weekdays including Bank Holidays 10 a.m. to 5 p.m. Closed Sundays. Admission 1/6d. Children 9d. Services free.

SCIENCE MUSEUM, Exhibition Road, SW7. (Tube to South Kensington.) Open weekdays including Bank Holidays 10 a.m. to 6 p.m. Sundays 2.30 to 6 p.m. Admission free.

SIR JOHN SOANE'S MUSEUM, 13 Lincoln's Inn Fields, WC2. (Tube to Holborn.) A unique collection representative of eighteenth-century taste in the arts, archaeology, etc., including Hogarth's famous *Marriage à la mode* series. Open Tuesday–Saturday 10 a.m. to 5 p.m. Closed during August. Admission free.

TOWER OF LONDON ARMOURIES, EC3. (Tube to Tower Hill.) Open weekdays including Bank Holidays 10 a.m. to 4 p.m. (From May to October open till 5 p.m.) Closed Sundays. Admission free Saturdays and Bank Holidays; other times—adults 6d. Children 3d.

VICTORIA AND ALBERT MUSEUM, Cromwell Road, SW7. (Tube to South Kensington.) One of the finest museums of its kind anywhere in the world, dealing with architecture, painting, sculpture, engravings, printing, ceramics, metalwork, textiles, etc. Open weekdays including Bank Holidays 10 a.m. to 6 p.m. Sundays 2.30 to 6 p.m. Admission free.

See also APSLEY HOUSE, CARLYLE'S HOUSE, DICKENS' LONDON (for Dickens' house), JOHNSON'S LONDON (for Johnson's house), and KEATS' HOUSE.

MUSIC. London is now richer in music than ever before, its orchestras sounder, its concert halls fuller. The Royal Festival Hall on the South Bank has proved extremely popular with concert-goers. The Proms are at the Royal Albert Hall from July to September. Opera can be heard at Covent Garden and at the Sadler's Wells theatre (see THEATRES). You will find times and dates of concerts listed in the Saturday editions of *The Times* or the *Daily Telegraph* or in *London Musical Events*—a month's programmes in advance for 1/-, published on the 22nd of each month, as well as—for big occasions—in the classified columns of the evening papers. Listed below are some of the more important halls, and how to get there.

Aeolian Hall, New Bond Street, W1 (MAY 4775). Tube to Bond St. or No. 25 bus.

People's Palace, Mile End Rd. E1 (ADV 3520). Tube to Mile End, thence trolleybus.

Royal Albert Hall, Kensington Gore, SW7 (KEN 8212). Nos. 9, 73, or 52 buses.

Royal Festival Hall, South Bank, SE1 (WAT 3191). See FESTIVAL HALL for details.

Wigmore Hall, Wigmore St. W1 (WEL 2141). Tube to Bond St. or Nos. 59, 159 or 113 buses.

N

NATIONAL MARITIME MUSEUM, Greenwich, SE10. (For how to get there and times of opening see under MUSEUMS.) A fascinating exhibition of nautical history, housed in part of the Royal Naval College. The original part, built by Wren, is by the river, and as the College extended, it took over the Queen's House on higher ground behind, which was designed by Inigo Jones for Anne, James I's Danish wife. If you want a gull's-eye view of Britain's greatness at sea, don't miss it.

NELSON'S COLUMN [E4] Trafalgar Square, WC2. One hundred and eighty-five feet high including the Admiral's own sixteen feet, it is made of Devon granite, and was finished in 1845. The reliefs around the base show Nelson's victories, and are cast from captured French cannon. Landseer's four lions have been lying there at the corners since 1867, looking more and more bored all the time. See TRAFALGAR SQUARE.

NEWSPAPERS. London has eleven morning newspapers, three evening and nine Sunday newspapers. The dailies and Sundays all have national distribution (biggest— *News of the World*, with over eight million circulation) and the evenings are read over wide areas of the Home Counties and the South Coast. See also FLEET STREET.

MORNINGS

Independent
 The Times, Printing House Square, EC4   CEN 2000

Conservative
 Daily Telegraph, Fleet St. EC4   CEN 4242
 Daily Express, Fleet St. EC4   CEN 8000
 Daily Mail, Northcliffe House, EC4   CEN 6000
 Daily Sketch, Kemsley House, WC1   TER 1234

Liberal
 News Chronicle, 13 Bouverie St. EC4   CEN 5000

Labour
 Daily Herald, Long Acre, WC2   CEN 1200
 Daily Mirror, Fetter Lane, EC4   HOL 4321

Communist
 Daily Worker, 75 Farringdon Rd. EC1   HOL 9242

EVENINGS

Conservative
 Evening Standard, 47 Shoe Lane, EC4   CEN 3000
 Evening News, Northcliffe House, EC4   CEN 6000

Liberal
  Star, Bouverie Street, EC4   CEN 5000

SUNDAYS

Independent
  Observer, 22 Tudor St. EC4   CEN 9481
  News of the World, Bouverie St. EC4   CEN 3030

Conservative
  People, 69 Long Acre, WC2   TEM 1200
  Sunday Times, Kemsley House, WC1   TER 1234
  Sunday Express, Fleet St. EC4   CEN 8000
  Sunday Graphic, Kemsley House, WC1   TER 1234
  Sunday Dispatch, Northcliffe House, EC4   CEN 6000

Labour
  Sunday Pictorial, Fetter Lane, EC4   HOL 4321
  Reynolds News, Wicklow St. WC1   TEM 6484

In addition to these, certain provincial dailies, notably
the *Manchester Guardian* and *The Scotsman*, have quite a
large circulation in London. And although, as its title
suggests, *The Financial Times* is concerned mainly with
money matters, it is read by many people as an ordinary
newspaper.

NIGHT CLUBS in London have suffered something of
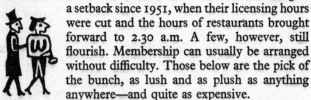
a setback since 1951, when their licensing hours
were cut and the hours of restaurants brought
forward to 2.30 a.m. A few, however, still
flourish. Membership can usually be arranged
without difficulty. Those below are the pick of
the bunch, as lush and as plush as anything
anywhere—and quite as expensive.

Astor, Fitzmaurice Place, Berkeley Square, W1 (GRO
3181). Entrance fee: £1; subscription: 10/6. Hours:
9 p.m.–4 a.m. Dancing from 10 p.m. Cabaret 1.15 a.m.
Cabaret Club, 16 Beak St. W1 (GER 4623, night GER
6862). Subscription: 1 guinea; entrance fee (after 10 p.m.):

£1. Hours: 7.30–3. Dancing from 8.30. Cabaret 10 and 1.

Calypso, 185 Regent St. W1 (REG 0557). Subscription: 1 guinea. No entrance fee, guests 12/6. Hours: 6.30–4. Dancing from 11. Cabaret 1.0

Coconut Grove, 177 Regent St. W1 (REG 7675, night REG 6897). Subscription 10/6; entrance fee £1. Hours: 9–4. Dancing from 10.30. Cabaret at 11 and 2.

Embassy, 6 Old Bond St. W1 (REG 5275). Subscription: 1 guinea. Hours: 8.30–4.30. Dancing from 9. Cabaret 12.30.

Four Hundred, 28 Leicester Square, WC2 (WHI 1813). Subscription: 5 guineas; entrance fee: £1. Hours: 9–4. Dancing from 10. No cabaret. Evening dress essential. The most exclusive night club. Membership applications carefully vetted.

Milroy, 5 Hamilton Place, W1 (GRO 5050). Subscription: 2 guineas; entrance fee: £1. Hours: 10.30–4. Dancing from 10.30. No cabaret.

New Churchill's, 160 New Bond St. W1 (REG 5934). Subscription: 1 guinea; entrance fee: £1. Hours: 6–4. Dancing from 10. Cabaret 1.15. Most popular all-round.

O

OFF-LICENCES are—as the name implies, if you work it out—places where you can buy beer, wine and spirits off, instead of on, licensed premises—in other words, liquor stores or wine merchants or beer shops, depending on your point of view. Sometimes attached to pubs but more often standing on their own, they supply you with anything you want to drink to take away, and usually operate normal shop hours. Off-licences attached to pubs usually manage to be able to sell during normal hours and when the pub is open as well. There's nothing, of course, to stop you from buying a bottle in a pub—the prices are just the same.

OLD BAILEY [G3] Newgate Street, EC4. (Tube to St Paul's.) 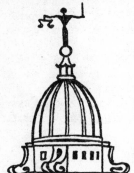Here, on the site of Newgate Prison, criminal cases are tried, as distinct from the civil cases (and criminal appeals) which are heard in the Royal Courts of Justice (see LAW COURTS).

You are allowed into the public galleries of the two Old Bailey courts at ten in the morning and two in the afternoon. You queue outside a little door in Newgate Street, and if no particularly juicy case is on, you should go there say half-an-hour before the doors open. Try to get into Number 1 Court, where you get a magnificent bird's eye view of the whole pomp and panoply of English justice from a gallery seat near the ceiling.

If you simply want to see over the building and not hear a case being tried, go to the entrance in the street called Old Bailey at eleven o'clock on Saturday morning, when there are people there to show you around.

OLD LADY OF THREADNEEDLE STREET. See BANK.

OLYMPIA, Hammersmith Road, W14. (Tube to Addison Road.) A great barn of a building used for exhibitions, circuses (Bertram Mills has his there every Christmas), horse shows, and a hundred and one other things.

OPEN AIR THEATRE. See REGENT'S PARK.

OPERA. See COVENT GARDEN and MUSIC.

OVAL. It you want to see cricket played in the true Cockney style, and are either awed or bored by Lord's, take the

Tube to Kennington Oval and go and sit in the shade of the gasometer and watch London's great south-of-the-river team, Surrey—traditional rivals of north London's Middlesex—move about the field in their ancient ritual with a freer grace and (perhaps) less self-consciousness. The cricket's the same, but there's a world of difference in the atmosphere.

OXFORD STREET [c4, d3 & e3] W1. London's mass shopping thoroughfare, stretching from Marble Arch to Tottenham Court Road in a straight busy line, it's the Mecca of suburban house-wives at sale time and its great stores do a vast volume of trade (for details, see SHOPPING).

With none of the dignity of Regent Street, no pretence at the *chic* of Bond Street, it's a cheery, chattering, take-it-or-leave-it old girl, decked out with neon lights and sales gimmicks, an old girl who has a warmth and a liveliness that her more respectable sisters haven't got.

P

PALL MALL [d & e 5] SW1. Running from the bottom of Regent Street up to St. James's Palace, somnolent and pompous, this with St James's, is clubland. Its name derives from the time when pell-mell, an early cross between cricket and croquet, was played here. Now the façades of the great clubs rise on either side with forbidding Victorian gentle-manliness. Bowler hats abound. And from behind the bleak tall windows, bald-headed men stare down at the sleepiness

below them, as though they were expecting something to happen.

PARKING. The parking problem has hit London worse, perhaps, than most other cities. For the charm of an unplanned town whose central streets have stayed more or less unchanged since the eighteenth and nineteenth centuries dissolves sometimes, as the traffic stalls and snarls, often because both sides of a narrow street are lined with parked cars. Watch yourself carefully if you're a stranger to London and have your car with you. The police are strict about parking anywhere, and there are forbidden areas marked with yellow bands on lamp posts and on the kerb: don't park beyond the yellow arrow. In a number of streets, the one-side-only, change-every-day parking rule applies. If you have a lot of calls to make around the town, do what many Londoners do—leave your car at home and go by bus or Tube or taxi. You'll find it simpler in the end.

PAWNBROKERS. I hate to mention it, but if you do run out of money, three well-known and reliable pawnbrokers are: Vaughan's, 39 Strand, WC2; T. M. Sutton, 156 Victoria Street, SW1; Jay Attenborough, 142 Oxford Street, W1.

PETTICOAT LANE [J & K3] Middlesex Street, E1. (Tube to Aldgate.) An Oriental street bazaar has nothing on this swarming market. Go there on a Sunday morning around eleven o'clock. In the narrow packed streets you can buy a year's supply of cough mixture, lock-knit ladies' underwear, an Alsatian dog in alabaster, a smoked herring, a canary, a radio set, a flowering shrub, a drape-cut suit, a bowl of jellied eels, a sink scourer or a suite of bedroom furniture.

You will see the true, live heart of the commercial East End—hucksters, mock auction men, barrow-boys and their girl friends, tailors' cutters from Aldgate on a Sunday morning walk with their wives, strong men breaking chains across their chests, direct descendants of the Artful Dodger, pearly kings, young marrieds from Kensington trying to find something amusing for the living-room.

It's an ideal way to spend a Sunday morning. The atmosphere is midway between that of a Mediterranean carnival and Saturday night at the dogs.

PHOTOGRAPHERS. You can go and have your photograph taken at lots of places. Most big stores, for example, have a special department. If you really feel like splashing out (and incidentally being made to look very glamorous), there are a number of very good (and expensive) society photographers such as:

Baron, 2 Brick St. W1		GRO 4441
Harlip, 161 New Bond St. W1		REG 3666
Pearl Freeman Ltd. 4 Berkeley St. W1		MAY 3871

If you want a passport type photograph, Polyfoto's do them, as well as their sheets of 48 photographs from which enlargements can be made.

Three of their branches are at:

    124 Baker St. W1
    61a Brompton Rd. SW3
    27 Kensington High St. W8

PHOTOGRAPHIC SHOPS AND SERVICES. For photographic supplies and developing and printing, there are plenty of places to go to. Below are just a few of the most reliable:

Boots (developing and printing only):

182 Regent St. W1	REG 4934
219 Piccadilly, W1	WHI 4761
25 Brompton Rd. SW1	KEN 6557

Kodak Ltd.

Kingsway, WC2	HOL 7841
184 Regent St. W1	REG 4657

R. G. Lewis Ltd.
   202 High Holborn, WC1   CHA 5954
   125 Strand, WC2   TEM 1405

Wallace Heaton Ltd.
   45 Berkeley St. W1   GRO 2691
   127 New Bond St. W1   MAY 7511

PICCADILLY [c5, d4 & 5] unrolls its aristocratic length

from its junction with Regent Street, Shaftesbury Avenue and Coventry Street at Piccadilly Circus (see EROS), to Hyde Park Corner. It opens at the Circus end in a bustle of big stores and specialist shops, and becomes slowly more aristocratic as it sweeps past the Ritz, and holds in its left hand Green Park and in its right clubs like the Army and Navy (known as the In and Out because of the large signs on its gate posts) and the Royal Aero Club, drawing up with a flourish as Park Lane saunters down to meet it by Hyde Park Corner. A lovely street to stroll along on a sunny morning, it contains the whole of London's West End in its almost-a-mile of stateliness, a blend of grey stone and shop window, grass and cab-ranks, spivs and sporting peers, hotels and harness-makers; and although it's getting on in years now, its heart is as strong as ever.

PLEASURE GARDENS, Battersea. (Buses Nos. 137, 19, 39, 45, 49, or by river ferry service from Westminster, Charing Cross, and Cadogan—Chelsea's Albert Bridge—Piers.) Laid out for the Festival of Britain, Battersea's Coney Island fulfils a long-felt London need. Acres of dodgems, roundabouts, coconut shies, and giant dippers, interspersed with elaborate fountains and theatres and lawns, may not be everybody's cup of tea, and seem to many of us to be too self-consciously gay to be really English. But the Pleasure Gardens have proved surprisingly popular since their opening and, subject to L.C.C. approval, they will go on opening every summer. If you've the time, go and make yourself feel pleasantly sick on the roundabouts first, but not too sick to enjoy a meal at the delightful riverside restaurant, where you can dine as the night comes down over the river and the tugboats and barges go drifting past with their red and green lights mirrored in the water.

POLICEMEN. Long the target for flattering remarks by visiting film stars, the Metropolitan (and City) police have earned the right to be called 'wonderful' by a deliberateness of gait, a slow helpfulness of manner and a near-divine sense of dignity. Impossible to shock or ruffle, you'll find them, even in the most unlikely circumstances, your friends.

Their West End headquarters are in Savile Row, inside whose cells many a young man later to become a Cabinet Minister, a Bishop or a High Court judge, has enjoyed a hot strong cup of tea on Boat Race Night, or some similar occasion. See also BOBBY and SCOTLAND YARD.

POST OFFICES. The British postal system is one of the most efficient in the world. Even post office pens—a standard pre-war joke—have improved during the last few years. There will be a post office quite near you, wherever you are, and any passer-by will be able to tell you where it is. They close at six o'clock, but two: London Chief Office, King Edward Street, EC1 (MON 9876)—near St

Paul's Tube Station, and Leicester Square Branch Office, 39 Charing Cross Road, WC2 (GER 2929)—towards Trafalgar Square from Leicester Square Tube Station—never close at all, and are open all night, Sundays included. There is a postbox half-way down Fleet Street, on the corner of Whitefriars Street, where the last collection (for next day's first delivery) is at 3 a.m. You'll find the telephone system operated by the General Post Office pretty efficient, too. Dial TEL for inland telegrams; 557 for overseas cables; CON for continental telephone calls; INT for other overseas calls; DIR if you know someone's name and address and want to know their number; TIM if you want to know the time; TOL or TRU for toll or trunk calls (toll short and trunk long distances from London); wake yourself up in the morning by dialling O the night before and asking the operator to give you a call. And dial O anyway if there's anything you don't quite understand; you'll find that nine out of ten operators are helpful and courteous and have a sense of humour.

PROMENADE CONCERTS. For details of the Proms, started by the late Sir Henry Wood almost two generations ago at the blitzed Queen's Hall in Langham Place, see ALBERT HALL and MUSIC.

PUBS. The pub, despite the growing pull of television, and the counter-attractions, at both profane and sacred levels, of the cinema and the church, still remains in London, just as everywhere else, the social focus for the little district which gives it its customers. It's no good writing about them; you must go and see for yourself. And you've a vast variety to choose from, ranging from the great gin palaces, glittering with cut-glass mirrors and bedecked with carved wood and moulded plaster, of Victorian London, that you'll find in Camden Town and Paddington and the Euston Road—all the older swallowed-up suburbs—to the quiet little single-roomed mews pub, once a coachman's taproom, and now very *chic*. Or there are a score of lovely riverside pubs stretching from Wapping to Kew where you can take your drink outside on a summer's evening and watch the Thames slide by. Or there are the early morning pubs which open at dawn in the great markets, where the porters drop in for a pint after their first couple of hours' work. Oh—to describe them all would be to write about every pub in London. And delightful as that would be, it's impossible. The standard drink remains beer; bitter or mild, light or dark, bottled or draught, we're drinking as much of it as ever. Gin-and-tonic is the favourite short drink; and now that Scotch is back in the bars, whisky-and-soda is once more the drink of the man with a bit of money.

Just a very few of the pubs that I like and that you might like to have a look at are listed below. There's not one that's the same as any of the others. So just drop in and have one with me.

WEST END

Antelope, Eaton Terrace, SW1
Coach and Horses, Avery Row, W1
De Hems, 11 Macclesfield St. W1
Dog and Duck, Frith St. Soho
Dover Castle, Weymouth Mews, W1
Fitzroy, corner of Windmill St. and Charlotte St. W1
Grenadier, Wilton Row, SW1
Hole in the Wall, Strand, WC2
Lord Belgrave, Whitcombe St. WC2
Mother Redcap, Camden Town (opposite Tube Station).
Nag's Head, Kinnerton St. SW1
Nag's Head, Covent Garden, WC2
Red Lion, Waverton St. W1
Salisbury, St. Martin's Lane, WC2
Shepherd's, Shepherd Market, W1
Villiers, Villiers St. WC2
Volunteer, Baker St. NW1 (opposite Regent's Park gates)
York Minster, Dean St. W1 (known as the French Pub)

CITY AND EAST END

Cheshire Cheese, Fleet St. EC4 (No. 145)
Cock, Fleet St. EC4 (No. 22)
George and Vulture, 3 Castle Court, EC3
Hoop and Grapes, 47 Aldgate High St. EC3
King Lud, Ludgate Circus, EC4
King's Head and Mermaid, 116 Lower Thames St. EC3
Pimm's, 3 Poultry, EC2
Punch Tavern, Fleet St. EC4

RIVERSIDE

City Barge, Strand-on-the-Green, Chiswick
Doves, Upper Mall, Hammersmith, W6
Prospect of Whitby, Wapping Wall, E1

CHELSEA

Cross Keys, Lawrence St. SW3
King's Head and Eight Bells, Cheyne Row, SW3

OUT-OF-THE-WAY

Bull and Bush, North End Way, NW3
Jack Straw's Castle, Hampstead Heath, NW3
Scarsdale Arms, Edwardes Square, W8
Spaniards Inn, Hampstead Heath, NW3
Windsor Castle, Campden Hill, W8

WINE BARS

El Vino's, Fleet St. EC4
Gordon's, Villiers St. WC2
Henekeys, 37 Thayer St. W1 (and other branches)
Layton's, 2a Duke St. W1
Shirreff's, 15 Great Castle St. W1
Short's, 333 Strand, WC2 (and other branches)

Q

QUEEN MARY'S ROSE GARDEN. See RE-GENT'S PARK.

R

RACE MEETINGS. There are many attractive race-courses on the outskirts of London. Ascot, Epsom, Kempton Park, Hurst Park, Sandown Park, Windsor and Lingfield Park are all within an hour or so of town. Try to go to one of the great meetings—the summer meeting at Epsom, with the Oaks and the Derby in the first week of June, or Royal Ascot in mid-June. Excursions are always run from the appropriate main line stations. For details of meetings, see the morning papers or (for fuller information) the mid-day editions of the evening papers, or the specialised racing publications like *Sporting Life*. Newmarket is a bit further away than the others, but it's still easily reachable from Liverpool Street. Alexandra Park, the Cockney's own race-course, has delightful little summer meetings (see ALEXANDRA PARK).

Both totalisator and bookmakers are available at all courses, and you can take your pick. Entrance charges tend to be high, so start off, at least, with plenty of money in your pocket.

RAILWAY STATIONS. The rule for the main line termini goes, with very few exceptions, like this:

TO EAST AND NORTH-EAST

	Enquiries
King's Cross	TER 4200
Liverpool Street	BIS 7600
Marylebone	PAD 3400

Cannon Street	WAT 5100
Charing Cross	,, ,,
London Bridge	,, ,,
Victoria	,, ,,
Waterloo	,, ,,

TO NORTH-WEST

Euston	EUS 1234
St Pancras	TER 3600

TO WEST

Paddington	PAD 7000

TO THE CONTINENT

Victoria	WAT 5151

RECORD SERVICES. If you want to find out about your family tree, or how many times your great-great-grandfather was married, talk to the Society of Genealogists, Chaucer House, Malet Place, WC1 (EUS 3330), who will search through their marriage index, which holds six million names covering most of the country from 1538 to 1837, and charge you only 7/6 an hour for finding out whether you are related to a duke or not.

Full official records of births, deaths and marriages are kept at Somerset House in the Strand. Searches are made for a nominal fee, and you can buy a copy of any certificate you like.

REGENT STREET [D3 & 4, E4] W1. Running from Carlton House Gardens up to Langham Place, and embracing Piccadilly Circus and Oxford Circus, Regent Street is perhaps the greatest shopping mile in the world. Originally designed by Nash for the Prince Regent, who wanted to have an impressive roadway from Carlton House to his proposed palace in Marylebone (which was never built), it achieved its proud swinging curve by accident: even the Prince could not buy up enough property to give himself the straight line he wanted, so Nash, rising above the difficulty, swung his plan round the obstacle to create the gracious sweep we know today.

The very best class of London's shops flank the street on either side. Household name after household name follow each other for a mile (see SHOPPING), and you can buy anything here from a golf ball to a ball gown.

REGENT'S PARK [B & C 1 & 2]. Stretching from Baker Street northwards to Camden Town, Regent's Park is a green and growing opening in London's streets and stone, only rivalled in popular favour by Hyde Park. The lake at the Baker Street end possesses rowing boats, canoes and ducks. Feeding ducks is, after all, one of the more satisfying things in life, and those I feed on the edge of the Regent's Park lake seem particularly pleasing.

Cross over the iron bridge and walk up over the Inner Circle road. On your left, past the tea gardens, is the OPEN AIR THEATRE (WEL 2060) which gives enchanted performances of *A Midsummer Night's Dream* and other Shakespearian comedies during the summer season. Performances are at 7.30, with matinees on Wednesdays, Thursdays and Saturdays at 2.30. To the right are QUEEN MARY'S ROSE GARDENS, with a breath-taking display of roses at the right time of year, and a gracefully laid-out artificial lake, complete with water lilies, weeping willows and an island rockery joined to the shore by a little wooden bridge.

Walk northwards from here for ten minutes and on Saturday afternoons you can watch a dozen games of cricket or football at the same time, see in the distance the brown rocks of Monkey Hill in the Zoological Gardens, which border on to the Park (see ZOOS), and hear an elephant's trumpeting mingled with the shrillness of a referee's whistle. Then swing back southwards, and walk alongside the old ship canal, now quietly asleep under the high interlacing trees, and so round the southern side of the lake, out into Baker Street again. *The Volunteer* awaits you on the right hand corner if you're thirsty; and just a few yards past it on the same side, is the computed site of 221b (now an office building), where Sherlock Holmes took tea and crumpets, smoked his pipe, wore his dressing-gown, played his violin and amazed Dr Watson.

RELIGIOUS SERVICES. See Churches.

RESTAURANTS. See DINING CLUBS, EATING OUT and TEA ROOMS.

RIDING. Although the internal combustion engine has

 driven the horse from the streets, there are still plenty of places in London where you can have a horse kept at livery or hire one to ride. Below are just a few of the most reliable riding schools and stables.

Cadogan Riding School, 87 Cadogan Lane, WS1 (SLO 8201). 16/6 per hour. Livery stables. Good with children.

Miss Lilo Blum, 32 Grosvenor Crescent Mews, SW1 (SLO 6846). 15/- per hour. Livery stables. Horses to ride or drive. Behind St George's Hospital.

Knightsbridge Riding School, 34 Queen's Gate Mews, SW7 (WES 8474). 10/6 per hour. 12/6 Sundays. Lessons 15/-. Near Albert Hall. Livery stables. Children and learners.

Hampstead Heath Riding Academy, 23a Downshire Hill, NW3 (HAM 0800). 10/6 per hour. 12/6 Sundays. 15/- lesson. ten lessons £6 10/-. No livery stables. Tube to Hampstead.

Epping Forest. Snaresbrook Riding School and Club, Woodford Road, Snaresbrook (WAN 3256). 9/- per hour including lesson. 15/- two hours. £1 10 0 per day. Riding in Epping Forest. Horses for shows, gymkhanas, etc. Tube to Snaresbrook. No. 720 Green Line.

Roehampton. Lester Riding Establishment, High St. Roehampton (PUT 6070). 7/6 per hour unescorted. 10/6 per hour escorted. Week ends 10/6. Livery stables. No. 30 bus from Kensington. Nos. 85 and 72 to the door.

RIVER BUSES AND TRIPS. We often forget that for centuries the Thames was London's main thoroughfare. It was the means of connecting the City, London's centre of gravity for well over a thousand years, built around the old Roman Forum and Temple (the sites of Leadenhall Market and St Paul's respectively), with the relatively late rival centre formed when the Court took up residence at the Palace of Westminster. Until the end of the first quarter of the nineteenth century, thousands of wherries plied for hire on the river, and the shout was 'Oars', not 'Taxi'. The horse omnibus, the first local railways (developing into the Tube), the tram, and finally, the motor bus, emptied the Thames of its little boats. Various attempts were made to revive it as a passenger highway, but they all failed until in 1948 a new generation found the experimental water buses an agreeable means of getting about. Since then, these buses have flourished. They operate from mid-April to the end of October at half-hourly intervals, from roughly 8 a.m. to 8 p.m. They run from Charing Cross Pier, connecting Putney with Greenwich, and calling at Wapping, Cherry Garden, and Tower Bridge, Lambeth and Chelsea.

These are truly river buses—a means of getting from one place to another. From Westminster Pier, other boats shuttle backwards and forwards with guides on board to show you London from London's main artery. Every twenty minutes, for example, there's a trip down to Tower Bridge and back, which takes from forty to fifty minutes—

the best possible way to see why London has taken the shape that it has. From here, too, you can go to Greenwich (every twenty minutes up to six o'clock); Richmond and Kew (every thirty minutes up to half-past five); and Hampton Court (every half-hour up to half-past one).

From Tower Pier, there's a day trip every weekday except Friday, from Whitsun until mid-September, which goes to Southend, Margate, Ramsgate and Clacton—London's nearest seaside resorts. The steamers leave shortly before nine in the morning. For details, apply to Eagle Steamers, 15 Trinity Square, EC3 (ROY 4021).

ROOSEVELT MEMORIAL. See GROSVENOR SQUARE.

ROWTON HOUSES. Headquarters: 17 Buckingham Palace Gardens, SW1 (SLO 5271). There are several blocks of these in various parts of London, where you can obtain a rough but clean bed for the night for practically nothing. The Ritz of the tramp, the idea is a typically late Victorian one.

ROYAL ACADEMY [D4] Burlington House, Piccadilly, W1. Founded in 1768, with Sir Joshua Reynolds as its first President, the Academy is best known for its annual Summer Exhibition, a selection by a committee formed from its forty-two academicians of contemporary work.

It also gives scholarships and free tuition to outstanding students, and generally promotes the visual arts (see BURLINGTON HOUSE).

ROYAL ARTILLERY AND MACHINE GUN CORPS MEMORIAL [C5] Hyde Park Corner. Jagger's famous and sombre World War I memorial dominates the traffic at Hyde Park Corner.

ROYAL AUTOMOBILE CLUB [D5] Pall Mall, SW1 (WHI 2345). Rival and partner of the Automobile Association (see AUTOMOBILE ASSOCIATION), it offers much the same services and is a very good alternative.

ROYAL COURTS OF JUSTICE. See LAW COURTS and OLD BAILEY.

ROYAL EXCHANGE [J4] Cornhill, EC3. (Tube to Bank.) The present very permanent-looking building is the third to have existed on the site since the first Elizabeth established the Exchange as a meeting-place for merchants. The grasshopper weather-vane on top comes from the coat of arms of Sir Thomas Gresham, which decorated the original building. Outside, the Duke of Wellington, astride a horse without a saddle, surveys the bustle of the City with stern misgiving, without, for some reason that is lost to us, having bothered to put his shoes on.

The Royal Exchange is now the headquarters of a large assurance company, and the official business of the Exchange is carried on behind closed doors at other places in the City. But its old status as the City's heart is still remembered at times of rejoicing or of crisis; new sovereigns are proclaimed, and wars declared, from the Royal Exchange steps.

ROYAL FESTIVAL HALL. See FESTIVAL HALL.

ROYAL OBSERVATORY, Greenwich Park, SE10. Although the real work of the Royal Observatory has now been transferred to Hurstmonceux in Sussex, Greenwich Mean Time is still telegraphed to all important towns at one o'clock in the afternoon, when the time ball on the eastern turret descends. And just a few yards north of the gates of the Observatory (built by Charles II), you can stand on the Zero Meridian of Longtitude, for when the first scientific maps of the modern age were being made, it was Greenwich that led the way to the world.

ROYAL SOCIETY [D4] Burlington House, Piccadilly, WI. Incorporated by charter in 1662, the Royal Society exists to further the advancement of scientific knowledge. The list of its members since its formation is an honour roll of British science. Papers by members are read regularly, and a collection of them is published yearly. The right to put F.R.S.—Fellow of the Royal Society—after your name is highly prized.

ROYAL STANDARD. The standard of the sovereign, which carries the royal coat of arms, in which heraldic insignia of the counties of Great Britain are incorporated, flies over Buckingham Palace when the Queen is in residence.

RUGBY FOOTBALL. See ANNUAL EVENTS and FOOTBALL.

S

ST JAMES'S PALACE [D5] SWI. Originally founded by Edward I as a hospital for fourteen leprous virgins, Henry VIII decided that it would be an excellent site for a hunting box in which to refresh himself while riding over the recently appropriated Manor of Hyde (see HYDE PARK). A palace was built to his orders in 1532, and although it has ceased to be a royal residence, the British Court is still officially the Court of St James, and ambassadors' credentials are written to that effect.

You can walk straight in through Clarence Gate in the Mall and wander through the courtyards. Here you can see the balcony where, in accordance with the Palace's official standing, a proclamation is read at the beginning of a new reign, and at the end of an old. The Palace is now used by Court officials. Services in the CHAPEL ROYAL on Sunday are open to the public. As you wander about, find Ambassadors Court, and go through the archway into Pall Mall. Cross over and walk up Crown Passage, a sleepy little backwater of old London, into ST JAMES'S, where the great clubs are flanked by little shops with proud histories (and often unspoilt façades): hat-makers, boot-makers, carriage-makers, fishing-tackle-makers, wine merchants. Across the road are the offices of the British Travel and Holidays Association. Straight ahead is Piccadilly.

And in case you're thinking that he was a hard man to turn them out in the snow, you should know that Henry VIII gave all the leprous virgins pensions.

ST JAMES'S PARK [D & E 5] London's most elegant

park spreads its formal walks and gardens over nearly a hundred acres between Whitehall and Buckingham Palace. It was originally laid out by Charles II, who also tried to dandify Hyde Park, but Nash did it over in 1828 and has left us a perfect example of Regency landscaping. Its lake is one of the loveliest in the world, and is a sanctuary for wild fowl, which include pelicans recently flown from America, symbols of a world that's changing even here: the first pelicans were given to Charles II by the Russian ambassador.

Stand on the bridge across the lake to see one of London's most magical vistas: the improbably romantic pinnacles of Whitehall Court in the background, and nearer to you, the War Office and Horse Guards Parade.

ST PAUL'S CATHEDRAL [H4] Ludgate Hill, EC4.

(Tube to St Paul's.) London has worshipped here ever since the first Roman Temple arose on a bare hill. St Paul's is probably the fifth building to have stood on the site. It was built by Wren to replace the Norman cathedral that was burnt down in the Great Fire of 1666. He was just forty-three when the first stone was laid and a dying man of seventy-seven when it was completed.

Here lie many of England's great men: Wren himself, and

Nelson and Wellington. Most Londoners only know St

Paul's from the outside as a landmark—the great dome surmounted by a golden ball and cross can be seen for miles in many directions. The blitz raged all round it, and St Paul's now stands miraculously preserved against a background of naked foundations and bombed sites. One large bomb fell only a few feet from the eastern wall and, failing to explode, was successfully removed by a bomb disposal squad, who won the nation's gratitude. The blitz, indeed, in opening up new vistas once hidden by the surrounding City buildings, has been kind to the Cathedral, even though it sustained a certain amount of incidental damage.

The best view of the Cathedral is from underneath the centre of the great dome, and the best view afforded by the Cathedral is from the stone gallery.

SCOTLAND YARD [E5] SW1. Properly New Scotland Yard, after the name of the little street which leads to the headquarters of the Criminal Investigation Department, and the Metropolitan Police, about a third of the way down Whitehall from Trafalgar Square on the left-hand side. The buildings, with delightful aptness, were constructed from granite hewn by Dartmoor convicts, and stand on the site of the old Palace of the Kings of Scotland. The Yard—as it is familiarly known—houses a Black Museum containing relics of headline crimes of the past, death masks of murderers, ingenious housebreaking instruments and so on. The only way to see it is to know someone in the Yard. The best way to do that is to strike up a conversation with any large, quiet man in a dark blue suit in one of the nearby pubs, expressing forceful admiration for the Metropolitan Police and the C.I.D.

SEASON, The. Beginning in May and running through to mid-July, the Season was once the only time of the year that many families came to London. Still the social climax of the year, it now runs to an established pattern, but since it concerns only a privileged few, it tends to be lost in the all-the-year-round rhythm of the capital. It's launched in early May with Queen Charlotte's Ball, the first of the great coming-out functions for debutantes, and swells through a round of parties and private balls, through Derby Day and Royal Ascot, Henley and Wimbledon, Eton and Harrow and the University Match at Lord's, St Andrew's Day at Eton and the ceremony of Trooping the Colour, Royal Garden Parties at Buckingham Palace, to a great June crescendo, fading away through July as town begins to empty of the rich and fashionable. All that it means to most Londoners is a sudden blossoming of young men in tail coats and grey top hats in the streets of Mayfair, the battle to be the debutante of the year, fought out in the gossip columns of the daily newspapers, the irruption of hundreds of shy girls with loud voices into a score of restaurants, and lines of venerable Daimlers and Rolls-Royces outside Claridges, and Browns and the Berkeley.

SECRETARIAL SERVICES. If you want to hire a secretary by the hour, day or week, three reliable firms, among many others, are:

Brook Street Bureau, 59 Brook St. W1	GRO 6666
Fine's Agency, 95/99 Praed St. W2	AMB 3400
Imperial Agency, 36 Dean St. W1	GER 6384

Most hotels make their own arrangements, and will supply you with a secretary if you ask them.

SHOPPING.

Of course, you can find everything in London. It's impossible to list here every conceivable item that you might want to buy, or even a hundredth of the shops you could buy them in. Below you will find just a few of the places

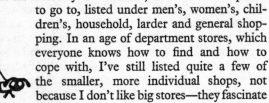

to go to, listed under men's, women's, children's, household, larder and general shopping. In an age of department stores, which everyone knows how to find and how to cope with, I've still listed quite a few of the smaller, more individual shops, not because I don't like big stores—they fascinate me—but because the small merchant is very much a part of the London tradition and, I hope, always will be.

MEN'S SHOPPING. London offers the finest of everything for the man and at all prices. Its tailoring, its shoes and shirts and hats, all are justly recognised to be the best in the world. For a window-shopping stroll, walk from the Piccadilly Circus end of Jermyn Street to St James's Street, down St James's and up the other side, cross Piccadilly into Bond Street and walk up as far as Oxford Street, then back again down the other side, left into Piccadilly, and left again at Piccadilly Circus up Regent Street to Oxford Circus. A longish stroll, but it will give you a fair idea of what the best shops are like. And in this aristocratic neighbourhood you'll find quite reasonable shops—chain-store branches and the like—side by side with shops as exclusive as any in the world. Below are some ideas which may help you:

Cigars. Go to the eighteenth-century shop of Messrs. Fribourg and Treyer, 34 Haymarket, SW1, for the right goods in the right atmosphere; or to any branch of any of the leading chain tobacconists like Lewis of Westminster, or the House of Bewlay.

Clothes for Hire. If you need a morning suit, a top hat, a dinner jacket, tails or skiing clothes, go to Moss Bros, 20 King Street, WC2. For fancy dress, go to M. Berman, 18 Irving Street, WC2, or L. & H. Nathan, 12 Panton Street, SW1.

Complete Outfitters. Austin Reed of Regent Street, and Simpson of Piccadilly are the best. Various chain stores like

Horne Brothers and Hope Brothers are also reliable. So are Harrod's and Selfridges. London's oldest outfitters are Thresher and Glenny, 152 Strand, WC2.

Hats. Go to Locks, 6 St James's Street, SW1, and choose your bowler correctly, just the right amount of curl and the right degree of hairiness, by allowing the assistant to give you what he thinks you ought to have. It's quite the best way. Go to Scotts, 1 Old Bond Street, or Dunn's, 24 Regent Street (at Piccadilly Circus), for something a little less extravagant. Both are very sound.

Pipes. Go to Dunhill's, 30 Duke Street, St James's, or one of the chain tobacconists.

Raincoats. Aquascutum, 100 Regent Street, or Burberry's, 18 Haymarket, SW1.

Safety Razors, Razor Blades, etc. From all chemists. Wilkinson's, 52a Pall Mall, SW1, are specialists.

Shirts. For ready-made shirts (far and away the more popular and quite a bit cheaper) the outfitters, or Morgan and Ball, 54 Piccadilly and branches. For made-to-measure (and London is supreme here): Hawes and Curtis, 2 Burlington Gardens, W1; Izod, 9 Hanover Square, W1; Sulka, 160 New Bond Street; Turnbull and Asser, 71 Jermyn Street, W1; Edouard & Butler, 15d Clifford Street, W1.; Philip Landau, 10 and 11 Moor Street, W1.

Shoes. The best hand-made shoes in the world come from Lobb, 26 St James's Street. McAfee, 38 Dover Street, W1, is another excellent bespoke shoemaker. For ready-made footwear, try the outfitters, or Russell and Bromley, 24 New Bond Street, or the Dolcis or Lotus shops.

Suits and Overcoats. The best suits in the world are made by a handful of bespoke tailors in London. A few of them are—and this can only be an arbitrary choice: Huntsman, 11 Savile Row, W1; Anderson and Sheppard, 30 Savile Row; Henry Poole, 37 Savile Row; Taylor and Gardiner, 30 Cork Street; Wyser and Bryant, 11 Princes Street, Hanover Square; Bailey and Weatherill, 89 Regent Street; Gieves, 27 Old Bond Street; Harry Hall, 235 Regent Street.

For ready-made suits and overcoats, go to the outfitters, or to Aquascutum, or Burberry's, or for something really reasonable and excellent value, try any of the branches of Montague Burton, or the Fifty Shilling Tailors.

Ties. Any of the good men's shops, really, but especially Turnbull and Asser, and Sulka.

Umbrellas, Shooting-sticks, Walking-sticks. For smart ones: Swaine, Adeney, Brigg, 185 Piccadilly. For not-so-smart: any Lost Property Sales Office.

Underwear. You get the best selection and choice at either Simpson's or Austin Reed.

Waistcoats. For the decorated and be-lapelled London waistcoat, go to Thomas Wing, 44 Piccadilly, or the little shops in Burlington Arcade.

Woollens. For really fine woollens and cashmeres, socks, pullovers, sweaters, etc., go to Jaeger, 204 Regent Street (who are also outfitters in the best London tradition), or Scott Adie, 29 Cork Street, W1.

WOMEN'S SHOPPING. You can get everything from a pin to a *peignoir* at any of the great department stores on the following list. Below them are a few other suggestions.

WEST END

Bourne & Hollingsworth, Oxford St. W1
Debenham & Freebody, 27 Wigmore St. W1
Dickins & Jones, Regent St. W1
D. H. Evans, 318 Oxford St. W1
Fenwick's, 63 New Bond St. W1
Fortnum & Mason, 181 Piccadilly, W1
Galeries Lafayette, Regent Street, W1
Jay's, 251 Regent St. W1
John Lewis, Oxford St. W1
Liberty, Regent St. W1
Marshall & Snelgrove, Oxford St. W1
Peter Robinson, Oxford Circus, W1
Robinson & Cleaver, 156 Regent St. W1
Selfridge's, Oxford St. W1

Swan & Edgar, Piccadilly Circus, W1
Walpole's, 87 New Bond St. W1

KNIGHTSBRIDGE AND VICTORIA

Army & Navy Stores, 105 Victoria St. SW1
Gorringes, Buckingham Palace Rd. SW1
Harrods, Brompton Rd. SW1
Harvey Nichols, Knightsbridge, SW1
Woollands, 95 Knightsbridge, SW1

KENSINGTON

Barkers, Kensington High St. W8
Derry & Toms, Kensington High St. W8
Pontings, Kensington High St. W8

CHELSEA

Peter Jones, Sloane Square, SW3

Accessories. For bags, belts, gloves, blouses, costume jewellery, scarves: Fior, 3-5 Burlington Gardens; Ships, 10a Berkeley Street. Also for belts and costume jewellery: Paris House, 41 South Molton Street, W1. For bags, also go to Asprey, 165 New Bond Street; Leatherluxe, 28 Old Bond Street. For scarves: Liberty's, Regent Street, and Jacqmar, 16 Grosvenor Street. For gloves: The Regent Glove Company, 239 Regent Street, and the White House, 51 New Bond Street. Also for belts and small leather goods, try Rowland Ward, 166 Piccadilly; for handbags and umbrellas, Susan, 68 New Bond Street.

Cosmetics. Big stores and chemists stock all standard lines, but for advice and beauty treatment, facials and so on, go to Elizabeth Arden, 25 Old Bond Street; Helena Rubenstein, 3 Grafton Street; Yardley, 33 Old Bond Street; Cyclax, 58 South Molton Street; and Gala of London, 48 Burlington Arcade.

Foundations. Big stores are best; but if you're a difficult size or want something special try: Illa Knina, 30 Bruton Street; Roussel, 137 New Bond Street; Spirella, Spirella House, Oxford Circus; Gino, 3 Newburgh Street, W1. MacMillan & Dorvidat, 17 Beauchamp Place, SW3.

Furs. London remains the traditional clearing-house for the world's fur trade. Just a few of the best furriers, in their various ways, are: Bradleys, Welbeck Street, W1; Maxwell Croft, Rosslyn House, 96 Regent Street; National Fur Company, 193–5 Brompton Road, SW3; Tico, 34 Grosvenor Street; Swears and Wells, 374 Oxford Street and branches; The Sheepskin Shop, 435 Oxford Street. The fur departments of Fortnum's and Harrods are also very good.

Hats. The millinery departments of Fortnum's, Harrods, and Harvey Nichols, and the Aage Thaarup cheap collection at Marshall and Snelgrove, and Galeries Lafayette are all reliable. If your ego needs something really lovely (and expensive) try: Aage Thaarup, 84 Brook Street, W1; Mirman, 9 Chesham Place; Rudolf, 54 Grosvenor Hill; Vernier, 32 George Street, W1; Erik, 51 Brook Street; Hugh Beresford, 26a Davies Street.

Jewellery. The best-known shops are: Cartier, 175 New Bond Street; Boucheron, 180 New Bond Street; Asprey, 165–9 New Bond Street; Goldsmiths and Silversmiths, 112 Regent Street. If you like antique adornment, go to Cameo Corner, 26 Museum Street, WC2, or try Richard Ogden in Princes' Arcade. For a repair that matters, go to Herring, Morgan and Southon, 9 Berwick Street, just by the street-market, who are cheap and quick.

Leather Repairs (handbags, etc.). Try Leatherluxe, 28 Old Bond Street.

Lingerie. If it's for a trousseau, and must be handmade go to Adele Davis, 10 New Bond Street; Lydia Moss, 17 Old Bond Street; Mary Richards, 13 Royal Arcade, Old Bond Street; but if you're in a hurry, you can find excellent things at Honore, 46 South Audley Street, and the White House, 51 New Bond Street.

Materials (Silks, Tweeds, Woollens). Liberty's and Jacqmar are excellent for silks. So is Gasmey, 33 Brook Street. Hunt and Winterbotham, 4 Old Bond Street, and Sefton Gray, 24 Brook Street, for tweeds, woollens and worsteds. John Lewis, D. H. Evans, and Dickins and Jones have good all-round material counters. Try too Allan's of 56 Duke Street, Grosvenor Square.

Outsize Fashions. It's wisest (I'm told) to stick to the outsize departments of the big stores, but have a look at one or two of the specialist shops like Netta, 95 New Bond Street, or Evans, 535 Oxford Street.

Shoes. If you want them handmade, try Hellstern, 11 Old Bond Street, Joseph Box, 61 Grosvenor Street or Gamba, 46 Dean Street, W1. Otherwise: Rayne, 58 New Bond Street; Delman, 16 Old Bond Street; Fanchon, 30 Old Bond Street; Russell & Bromley, 24 New Bond Street; Pinet, 47 New Bond Street; Lilley and Skinner, 358 Oxford Street; Dolcis, 86 New Bond Street; Lotus, 43 New Bond Street.

Stocking Repairs. Nearly all dry cleaners, and many big department stores, will invisibly mend your nylons. Otherwise, take them to the Invisible Mending Company, 6 Piccadilly (next to the London Pavilion), who, incidentally, mend all other garments, too.

Woollens. London is justly proud of her woollens. For cashmeres, try N. Peal, 54 Burlington Arcade; or Scott Adie, 29 Cork Street. For all kinds of woollens, try Hunt and Winterbotham; Jaeger; Huppert, 64 Regent Street; the White House; or Fortnum and Mason.

In your tours round London, you'll notice shops with several or many branches. Most of them are in expensive, and many of them are worth looking at. C. & A. Modes Ltd., 505 Oxford Street, have branches everywhere; Cresta Silks Ltd., 174 Regent Street, have branches in Sloane Street, Brompton Road, New Bond Street; Richard Shops, 180 Regent Street, have branches in all main shopping streets. And do, by the way, look in at any of the Marks and

Spencer stores. They're incredibly cheap, and very good value.

CHILDREN'S SHOPPING. You'll probably find all you want in the way of children's clothing in the big stores, but there are the specialist shops: Daniel Neal, 3 Portman Square, W.1; Gay Child, 36 South Molton Street; Lynne, 9 New Bond Street; Treasure Cot, 103 Oxford Street; (for boys) Rowes, 120 New Bond Street. For toys, go to Hamley's, 202 Regent Street, for several floors of everything a child could want. Harrods, and Heal's (196 Tottenham Court Road) have delightful toy departments. Bassett-Lowke's, 112 High Holborn, WC1, is the place to take the serious model (*not* toy) train enthusiast. Gamage's, 118–128 Holborn, EC1, is excellent for the older boy who's beginning to think about airguns.

SHOPPING FOR THE HOUSEHOLD

China and Glass. See CHINA and GLASS.

Household Articles. Try the cheap chain store branches like Woolworth's and Littlewood's. For your pots and pans and general fittings, try Staines, 94 Victoria Street (near Victoria Station). If you're looking for Continental gadgets, go to Soho—and look for the little shops that supply the foreign restaurants.

Household Linen. The White House will sell you lovely (but expensive) things. Other specialists: Givan's Irish Linen Stores, 111–114 New Bond Street; Walpole's, 87 New Bond Street; Robinson and Cleaver, 156 Regent Street.

Modern Furniture. If you don't like antiques (if you do, see ANTIQUES), and prefer something modern, try Liberty's, Regent Street, or Heal's, Tottenham Court Road, special modern furniture departments. Also worth visiting: Story's, 49 Kensington High Street, W8; Peter Jones, Sloane Square, SW3.

Pictures. See ART GALLERIES.

Prints. You'll find something that reeks of old London in any one of the following: Thomas H. Parker, 2 Albemarle

Street; E. Seligmann, 25 Cecil Court, Charing Cross Road; W. T. Spencer, 27 New Oxford Street, WC1; Medici Galleries, 7 Grafton Street; Ganymed, 10 Great Turnstile, WC1; Zwemmer Galleries, 26 Litchfield Street, WC2.

Radios, Television, Records. There's a large staff (including linguists) at His Master's Voice, 363 Oxford Street, to help you make your choice. For the discerning collector, there is nowhere better than Rimington Van Wyck, 42 Cranbourn Street, WC2, or E.M.G., 6 Newman Street, W1. If you want to hire a radio or television set, go and see R.A.P. Rentals, 121 Regent Street.

Rugs and Carpets. Try: A. Maurice, 78 Wigmore Street, for Persians (and repairs). Perez, 162 Brompton Road, SW3, has large stocks of Oriental and European carpets. Try also Liberty's, Harrods and Heal's.

Silver and Sheffield Plate. Try the Goldsmiths and Silversmiths Co.; Mappin and Webb, 172 Regent Street; Wilson and Gill, 139 Regent Street; or Leighton, 7–11 Burlington Arcade.

Timepieces. For clocks, watches (travelling or bedside or what-have-you) go to Asprey's, or Benson's, 25 Old Bond Street, both of them famous and wonderful. More modern and not so expensive: Tyme, 5 New Bond Street. For the collector: Percy Webster, 17 Queen Street, Mayfair.

SHOPPING FOR THE LARDER

London, of course, consists of lots of villages, and most of the time you buy your food in the nearest village street. Three big stores specialise in food: Fortnum and Mason, with their fabulous peaches in brandy, *pâte de foie gras*, and game pie, have an excellent provision shop, which will make your mouth water with its smell alone. If you're going out for the day, its picnic baskets are magnificent, though expensive. Harrods and Selfridge's both have excellent departments where you can buy everything. For Continental food, go to Soho (see DELICATESSENS).

For your wine, go to an off-licence if you want something cheap and simple, or, if you want something a little better, to one of London's many excellent wine merchants. Just a few of them are: Berry Brothers and Rudd, 3 St James's Street; Ling's of London, 5 Avery Row; Cockburn and Campbell, 26 Curzon Street; David Sandeman and Calrow, 64 Pall Mall; Findlater, Mackie, Todd, Wigmore Street; Saccone and Speed, 32 Sackville Street, W1; Block, Grey and Block, 26 South Audley Street.

SHOPPING GENERALLY

Just a few more ideas about shopping in general:

Binoculars and Spectacles. The exotically-named Negretti and Zambra, 122 Regent Street, will supply all your needs, and will even hire you binoculars for race meetings, as well as mend your glasses.

Cameras. See PHOTOGRAPHIC SHOPS AND SERVICES.

Confectionery For top-grade handmade, and utterly delicious chocolates, go to Charbonnel and Walker, 31 Old Bond Street; Bendick's, 151 New Bond Street; or the confectionery department of Fortnum and Mason. Sagnes, in Marylebone High Street, make excellent French pastries.

Gifts. For something for a girl friend go to Fior's in Burlington Gardens, or Paris House, where you'll be advised without giggles. Girls can buy male gifts at the Pewter Shop, 18 Burlington Arcade. But perhaps the best thing to do anyway is to wander up and down the Arcade and see just what delightful little things there are in all the windows: silver tooth-picks, knives with twenty-five blades, drinking flasks, chessmen, cashmere scarves and sweaters, sets of poker dice, fancy waistcoats.

Sports Equipment. For all kinds of sporting equipment, go to Lillywhite's, 24 Regent Street. It's a fascinating store and you can get everything there from a golf tee to a ski cap. Specialists are:

Cricket: Jack Hobbs Ltd. 59 Fleet Street, EC4.

Fishing tackle: Hardy Brothers, 61 Pall Mall; Westley Richards, 23 Conduit Street; Ogden Smiths, 62 St James's Street.

Riding Clothes: Harry Hall, 235 Regent Street; Champion and Wilton, 451 Oxford Street (saddles, whips, etc); Bernard Weatherill, 55 Conduit Street.

Sporting Guns: James Purdey, 57 South Audley Street; Henry Atkins, 88 Jermyn Street; Cogswell and Harrison, 168 Piccadilly; Stephen Grant and Joseph Lang, 7–8 Bury Street, St James's.

Tennis, Badminton and Squash Rackets: Gordon Lowe, 23 Brompton Arcade, SW3; John Holden, Ltd. 232 Baker Street, NW1; or Hamley's.

Yachting Equipment: Beale's, 194 Shaftesbury Avenue, W1.

Tartans. You need not go to Scotland for your tartan clothes or rugs: go to the Scotch House, 2 Brompton Road, SW1; and for more exotic Scottish impedimenta, to the Scottish Highland Industries, 31 Beauchamp Place, SW3.

Travel Goods. For really first-class leather suitcases and the like, try Drew and Sons, 33 Regent Street, or John Pound, 67 Piccadilly. For a second-hand bag or brief-case, go to any one of the Lost Property Sales Offices (see LOST PROPERTY).

SIGHT-SEEING. See TOURS.

SKATING. You can skate to your heart's content in London. Below are the more central ice and roller rinks.

ICE

Harringay, 4 Green Lanes, N4 (STA 8221). Also ice hockey. 2.30–5 p.m. and 7.45–10.15 p.m. Mondays, Thursdays, Fridays and Sundays 2/6. Piccadilly Line Tube to Manor House.

Earl's Court, Empress Hall, Lillie Road, SW6 (FUL 1212). Ice hockey matches on Sundays at 8 p.m. with skating afterwards. 3/9 at door, 6/-, 8/6, 12/6 bookable. Tube to West Brompton or Earl's Court, or Nos. 30, 31, and 74 buses.

Queen's Ice Skating Club, Queensway, Bayswater, W2 (BAY 0172). Restaurant, coaches, exhibitions. Members only, or guest with voucher signed by member. Annual subscription 1/-; to skate 3/-; spectators 1/6, except at week-ends, when the charge is 2/6. Hire of skates 1/6. 9.30-12 noon, 2-5 p.m., and 6.30-9.30 p.m. daily. 7-9.30 p.m. Sundays. Tube to Queen's Way, or 12 or 88 buses.

Richmond Sports-Drome, Richmond Bridge, Clevedon Road, Twickenham (POP 3646). Two rinks. Curling on Tuesday evenings. Adults 2/6. Hire of skates 1/-. Children 1/6. Hire of skates 6d. Mondays 10-12.15 p.m. 2.30-5 p.m. and 7-10 p.m. Tuesdays 10-12.15 p.m. 2.30-4.45 p.m. and 8-10 p.m. Wednesdays, Thursdays and Fridays 10-12.30 p.m. 2.30-5 p.m. and 7-10 p.m. Saturdays 10.30-12.30 p.m. 2.30-5 p.m. and 7-10 p.m. Sundays 10-12.30 p.m. 3-5.30 p.m. and 7.30-10 p.m. Tube to Richmond, or Nos. 27a, 90, 90b, 33, 37 buses.

Wembley Empire Pool, Wembley (WEM 1234). Also ice hockey on Thursdays at 7.45 p.m. 2/6, 5/-, 7/6, 12/6. One hour's free skating after match. Instructors available at 6/- for 20 minutes, 5/- or 4/-. Skating Monday-Friday 2.30-5 p.m. 7.30-10 p.m. except Thursday. Sunday 10-12.30 p.m., 2.30-5 p.m. and 7.30-10 p.m. 2/6. Hire of skates 1/6. Children 1/6 except Saturday and Sunday. Special Saturday morning class of instruction at 9 a.m. 2/6. Tube to Wembley Park.

ROLLER

Alexandra Palace, Wood Green (TUD 5000). Restaurant and bar. 7.30-10.30 p.m. weekdays, 7-10 p.m. Saturdays. 1/6 Monday-Thursday. 2/- Friday and Saturday. Club Sunday. 1/6 plus 1/6 entrance. Children 6d Saturdays at 10 a.m. 1/6 Saturdays at 2.30 p.m. Tube to Wood Green.

Brixton, 2 Tulse Hill, SW2 (TUL 4812). Closed Sundays. Monday–Thursday 2/-, Friday and Saturday 3/-. 2.30 p.m. and 7.30 p.m. Nos. 59a or 159 buses to Brixton, thence Nos. 3 or 37 buses to the *George Canning*.

Cricklewood, 194 Cricklewood Broadway, NW2 (GLA 1415). Monday–Friday 7 p.m. 1/6. Saturday and Sunday 3 and 7 p.m. 2/6 except Sunday evening 2/-.

SMITHFIELD MARKET [G3] EC1. (Tube to Farring-

don.) Meat may be on the ration, but you'll never believe it if you go to Smithfield off the Farringdon Road, which rises on the site of the old Bartholomew Fair. Here the meat is as red as the faces of the butchers—many of them still refulgent in the traditional dress of their calling: boater, white overall, and blue and white striped apron, with blood stains optional.

SOHO, W1. The district of

foreign restaurants, delicatessens, shady dives, film tycoons, spivs and spices, it gets its name from the old hunting cry to call hounds off—'So ho!'—which dates from the time when there was nothing here but green fields, a favourite spot for a day's sport with the gentlemen of Westminster.

Its cosmopolitan atmosphere started when the Huguenots settled there in the sixteenth century. Soho is enclosed in the square made by Charing Cross Road, Oxford Street, Regent Street, and Shaftesbury Avenue, but it spills over a little outside these boundaries, carrying its smells of roasting coffee and cooking down as far as Leicester Square in the South, and up to Percy Street and Charlotte Street in the north. Its grey decaying Georgian streets and squares have been turned to a thousand uses, and here you can buy pepper pots, musical instruments, a ticket for a boxing match, a chef's hat, foreign newspapers and magazines, and above all, every kind of food: Indian, Spanish, Turkish, French, Greek, Italian, Chinese, Hungarian, Jewish, German, Cypriot, even English. For details of restaurants, typical Soho pubs and provision stores, see EATING OUT, PUBS and DELICATESSENS.

SOMERSET HOUSE [F4] Strand, WC2. Built in 1547 on the south side of the Strand, it's now used to keep the records—births, marriages, deaths and wills—of the British people (see RECORD SERVICES).

SOUTHWARK CATHEDRAL [H5] (Tube to London Bridge). In the heart of the Borough stands Southwark Cathedral, jostled by street markets and memories. It's not as ancient as it looks—most of the old Cathedral was burnt down in the last century—but it stands on a site which goes far back into London's past. Its stained glass windows commemorate some of the great men associated with the district—Chaucer (nearby stood the *Tabard*, where the pilgrims assembled for their journey to Canterbury), Bunyan, Dr Johnson, Oliver Goldsmith. Incidentally, for American visitors, the Harvard Chapel commemorates the founder of Harvard University who was born in the parish in 1607. Near at hand, in a yard by a railway siding, is the *George*, London's last balconied inn.

SPEEDWAY RACING. Motor cycle racing on cinder tracks is a great and still-growing favourite with Londoners. The season is from Easter to October, and all tracks have meetings on weekdays and Saturdays. For details, see the classified columns of the evening papers. Leading London tracks are:

Harringay, Green Lanes, N4 (STA 3474). Tube to Manor House.

New Cross, Hornshay St. SE15 (NEW 0213). Tube to New Cross.

Wembley, Empire Stadium, Middlesex (WEM 1234). Tube to Wembley or Wembley Park.

West Ham, Custom House, E16 (ALB 2441). Tube to Plaistow, thence trolleybus.

Wimbledon, Plough Lane, SW17 (WIM 4248). Tube to Tooting Broadway, then trolleybus.

SPIV. No one is quite clear about the derivation of the word; all we know is that the war and its resultant black market produced a mutation from the normal breed, and we called it spiv. Immortalised on the stage by the late, great Sid Field's Slasher Green, with grotesquely padded shoulders, slouch hat, long lurid tie, pointed shoes and thin moustache, the spiv is disappearing with the controls that created him. You'll find a last few hardy representatives though, lounging about in Coventry Street on Saturday night, or waiting for the results of the 2.30 at the corner of Frith Street and Old Compton Street. If one of them approaches you with the password of his profession (a dramatic and yet intimate 'psssst!') and offers to sell you Big Ben, don't listen; it probably doesn't belong to him anyway.

STRAND [E & F 4] WC2. A bustling crowded street that runs from Trafalgar Square to Ludgate Circus, becoming Fleet Street at the City end, the Strand is one of London's oldest thoroughfares. It was once the land equivalent of the Thames, linking the old City to the new. People say that the course of the street is that taken by Boadicea (whose statue stands by Westminster Bridge) when she rode out in her chariot to do battle with the Roman invaders. Once a top-flight shopping centre, the Strand has suffered from the steady shifting of business and fashion westwards away from the City, and has the look of someone who has seen better times. At the end of the last century, it was the favourite Saturday night promenade for the poorer Londoner, and it's from then that 'Let's all go down the Strand (have a banana)' comes. Here, too, the emphasis has shifted westward to Piccadilly Circus and Coventry Street and Leicester Square.

SUNDAY. No, it *isn't* so dull on Sunday. Let's just think what there is to do. There's some magnificent choral singing and organ music in the churches; there are the street markets like Petticoat Lane and Club Row; there's Hyde Park with the Serpentine to mess about in or on during the summer, and all the year round the orators at Speakers' Corner; cinemas open at 4.30 with two complete programmes—the second one usually beginning at seven or half-past; there's a whole gamut of afternoon concerts (which are advertised in the Saturday papers); there are river trips; there's the echoing emptiness of the City to explore and wonder at; there's the ritual of the lunch-time drink at the local. For most Londoners, it means a late sloppy breakfast and the Sunday papers; then the Sunday lunch and forty winks in an armchair afterwards. For literally hundreds of thousands, it means the one day in the week when they can really get something done in the garden. And, nice thing, Sunday restfulness applies to newspaper sellers too: have you noticed the piles of unattended papers where you're trusted simply to take your paper and leave the right money? No, it's not dull; just a bit lazy. And thank heaven for that.

SPEAKERS' CORNER. See MARBLE ARCH.

SPORT. See EXERCISE and under the different sports.

T

TAXIS. London's taxicabs range from rickety old puffing-billies which seem (with their drivers) to be of pre-World War I vintage, to purring smoothies smelling of leather and metal polish. But they are all built to the same basic specifications which have stood the test of years. Their steering lock enables them to make a U turn in a narrow street; they can reach full acceleration in a yard or two and pull up in less. Cheapest ride (the first mile for 1/3) has gone up a  bit since the pre-war 6d for the first mile; but it still remains good value. There's no real shortage of cabs now at normal times, although of course on occasions—curtain time at theatres in the West End on a rainy night, for example—they are few and far between. With a little encouragement your taxi driver will quite often turn into a cicerone and friend; and you'll find no one better to show you London than a taxi driver who's feeling at peace with life. You won't get a better meal either than the one you'll get at a café your driver's prepared to recommend and take you to, or a better cup of tea. For the sort of tip you should give him, see TIPPING.

Cab ranks are listed in the telephone directory under 'Taxicab', and you can expect to get one on the telephone at most times during the day, but not usually late at night. A recent innovation is the fleet of a hundred or more Radio Cabs, controlled from a central operations room, by RT. You telephone TER 8800, give your name and address, and they will ring you back, if you ask them, when your driver reports that he is nearing your door. There's no extra charge for this service; increased efficiency pays for the operating overheads.

TEASHOPS. London is nearly as thickly packed with teashops as it is with pubs, a monument to our second national beverage. Most are branches of the big chains, Lyons, A.B.C. or Express Dairies. Here you can get excellent cheap meals at more or less any hour of the day. Apart from these, there are the cafés, often owned and operated by the guv'nor and his missus, who probably pronounce the word as 'cayff', and talk in terms of 'a nice hot cuppa'. Food here, less standardised and probably less clean, is liable to be excellent and appetising. At the other end of the scale are the smart tearooms of the West End, filled with women in hats looking at each other. Among the best-known is Gunters, at the Park Lane end of Curzon Street. Most big stores serve very good teas in their restaurants all through the afternoon, and so do most hotels.

TELEPHONE. See POST OFFICES.

TEMPLE. See INNS OF COURT.

TENNIS. See EXERCISE and WIMBLEDON.

THEATRE TICKET AGENCIES. You can get tickets for every kind of entertainment from a number of agencies for a nominal booking charge. Below are a few of the most reliable.

Ashton & Mitchell, 2 Old Bond St. W1	MAY 7222
Chappell & Co. Ltd., 50 New Bond St. W1	MAY 7600
Keith Prowse, 159 New Bond St. W1 (and branches)	REG 6000
Leader's Box Office, 14 Royal Arcade, W1	REG 0846
Theatre Tickets & Messengers Ltd. 100 St Martin's Lane, WC2	TEM 1023

There are also ticket agencies in most large hotels and stores.

THEATRES. London's theatre is flourishing. The diet

is rich and varied, and unless you are extraordinarily difficult to please, you should be able to find at least three or four shows running to suit your taste. Listed below are the leading West End theatres.

Adelphi, Strand, WC2	TEM 7611
Aldwych, Aldwych, WC2	TEM 6404
Ambassadors, West St. WC2	TEM 1171
Apollo, Shaftesbury Avenue, W1	GER 2663
Cambridge, Earlham St. WC2	TEM 6056
Casino, Old Compton St. W1	GER 6877
Coliseum, St Martin's Lane, WC2	TEM 3161
Comedy, Panton St. SW1	WHI 2578
Criterion, Piccadilly Circus, W1	WHI 3216
Drury Lane, Catherine St. WC2	TEM 8108
Duchess, Catherine St. WC2	TEM 8243
Duke of York's, St Martin's Lane, WC2	TEM 5122
Fortune, Russell St. WC2	TEM 2238
Garrick, Charing Cross Rd. WC2	TEM 4601
Globe, Shaftesbury Avenue, W1	GER 1592
Haymarket, Haymarket, SW1	WHI 9832
Hippodrome, Cranbourne St. WC2	GER 3272
His Majesty's, Haymarket, SW1	WHI 6606
Lyric, Shaftesbury Avenue, W1	GER 3686
New, St. Martin's Lane, WC2	TEM 3878
Old Vic, Waterloo Rd. SE1	WAT 7616
Open Air Theatre, Regent's Park, NW1	WEL 2060
Palace, Shaftesbury Avenue, W1	GER 6834
Palladium, Argyll St. W1	GER 7373
Phoenix, Charing Cross Rd. WC2	TEM 8611
Piccadilly, Denman St. W1	GER 4506
Prince of Wales, Coventry St. W1	WHI 8681
Princes, Shaftesbury Avenue, W1	TEM 6596
Royal Opera House, Covent Garden, WC2	TEM 7961
St James's, King St. SW1	WHI 3903
St Martin's, West St. WC2	TEM 1443
Saville, Shaftesbury Avenue, W1	TEM 4011
Savoy, Strand, WC2	TEM 8888
Scala, Charlotte St. W1	MUS 5731
Stoll, Kingsway, WC2	HOL 3703
Strand, Aldwych, WC2	TEM 4143
Vaudeville, Strand, WC2	TEM 4871

Victoria Palace, Victoria St. SW1	VIC 1317
Westminster, Palace St. SW1	VIC 0283
Whitehall, Trafalgar Square, SW1	WHI 6692
Windmill, Great Windmill St. W1	GER 7413
Winter Garden, Drury Lane, WC2	HOL 8881
Wyndham's, Charing Cross Rd. WC2	TEM 3028

FURTHER AFIELD

Embassy, Swiss Cottage	PRI 2211
King's, Hammersmith	RIV 5094
Lyric, Hammersmith	RIV 4432
Sadler's Wells, Rosebery Avenue, EC1	TER 1672

THEATRE CLUBS have been a feature of London's theatre life for many years, and it was through them that Ibsen first burst upon and astonished Victorian England. Nowadays, they tend to concentrate on problem plays and intimate reviews, and afford an excellent shop window in which new plays and new talent can be shown without backers being involved in heavy expenses. *The Players'* is a rule unto itself: a reconstruction of a nineteenth-century music hall, with ritual calls from a white-tied chairman to an audience that always contains enough *habitués* to make the correct ritual responses. You can have a drink while you watch the diversions proffered for your entertainment, and join in the choruses of the old songs. For membership of the clubs listed below, simply write to or telephone the Secretary.

Arts, 6 Great Newport St. WC2	TEM 3334
Boltons, Drayton Gardens, SW10	KEN 0433
Gateway, 103 Westbourne Grove, W2	BAY 1910
Irving, 17 Irving St. WC2	WHI 8657
New Lindsay, 81 Palace Gardens Terrace, W8	BAY 2512
New Torch, 50 Wilton Place, SW1	SLO 4424
Players', Villiers St. WC2	TRA 1134
Royal Court, Sloane Square, SW3	SLO 1745
Unity, Goldington St. NW1	EUS 5391
Watergate, 29 Buckingham St. WC2	TRA 6261

TIPPING. My impression is that there's less tipping in London than in most other capitals; but perhaps you always feel like that about your own home town. Certain rough rules may, in the one direction save you money, and, in the other, save you from the frowns of doormen and the like. In a restaurant (see EATING OUT) you should tip a rough ten to fifteen per cent of the total bill. In a bar, if you have drinks brought to your table, you should tip the same sort of amount. In really smart bars, it's customary to give a small tip to the barmen either with each round of drinks or at the end, even if you're at the bar. You should pay 6d in a cloakroom for leaving your hat and coat—pay it when you collect them, not when you leave them. You should pay 6d in a lavatory if you wash your hands or have a brush-down from the attendant, nothing if you don't (although I am reliably informed that the ladies should always pay a minimum of 6d). You should give a porter or doorman 6d if he calls you a cab, even if, in a lordly way, he just beckons one off the rank outside. If it's a filthy night, and he spends ten minutes looking, you should, of course, pay him more. In hotels, if you're only staying over-night, tipping is optional; but if you're staying any length of time, you should tip the chambermaid, the porters and so on, each separately, depending on the sort of service you've had from them—not less than a few shillings each. You should also tip for any room service. You should tip in a barber's shop and hairdresser's, say something like twenty per cent of the bill, provided you've had good service and want it again. At the odd parking site which provides a uniformed attendant, you should also tip—the attendant usually sees that you do—a shilling is ample.

Everyone has his own rules about taxis. 6d is the minimum, on fares up to about 3/-, and beyond that you can get away with a shilling for quite a bit. A thick fog, icy roads or particularly helpful conduct on the driver's part all call for a bit extra.

You should *not* tip in shops; nor should you tip the cinema attendant who shows you to your seat, or in a theatre (except possibly the programme girl if you can conquer your irritation at paying sixpence for a programme worth a farthing). You should tip a guide or usher who has taken time and trouble in showing you round a museum or art gallery or the like—1/- to half-a-crown depending upon the extent of his helpfulness. You should *not* tip a policeman for telling you the way to somewhere.

Obviously, these can only be general pointers towards the right kind of occasions and the right kind of amount to tip. You will still get service in London whether you tip or not, which is a pleasant thing to realise. And you will get no more service if you over-tip than if you tip correctly, which is equally pleasant.

TOURS. You can arrange a tour of London in several ways. First, there are the guides available from the British Travel and Holidays Association in St James's (see B.T.H.A.). Many Travel agencies, too, have special tour-organisers. The river is an excellent vantage point from which to view the whole sweep of the City, and regular trips run every day from Westminster Pier (see RIVER BUSES). Finally, London Transport operate regular bus tours during the summer. For details apply to travel agents or telephone ABB 1234. What better way to see the town than from the top of a red London bus, with a guide to tell you what's what?

TOWER OF LONDON [J & K 4] EC3 (Tube to Tower Hill). William the Conqueror

built the White Tower just outside the walls of the original town, in order to have a strongpoint from which he could keep an eye on the disgruntled Saxons, and have somewhere to retire to if the resistance groups began to turn ugly. They didn't; and his successors added to the fortress, dug moats, set up draw-bridge and portcullis, laid out walks and lawns. Kings lived there; enemies were imprisoned there; inconvenient people were beheaded there—including two of Henry VIII's wives, Anne Boleyn and Catherine Howard. A Royal Menagerie was formed and kept there; and the old black ravens that croak across the lawns, and are on the official ration strength of the Tower Guard, are its last survivors. And all this you can see today: the room where the Little Princes were imprisoned by their archetypal Wicked Uncle; the port-cullis, which still works, guarding the (so named to the delight of generations of schoolchildren) Bloody Tower; the Crown Jewels in the Wakefield Tower; the Armouries in the White Tower; the Chapel of St John, the oldest church in England where the Norman court worshipped.

The Tower is protected by forty-three Yeoman Warders, who still wear the uniforms designed for them by Henry VII, who recruited them in 1485. Ever since the Grand Duke of Tuscany wrote in the seventeenth century 'they are great eaters of beef', they have been known as BEEFEATERS.

It's the beefeaters who show you round, make sure you don't walk off with the Crown of State and feed the ravens. Times have changed since Henry VII's day. The Beefeaters get no more beef than anyone else; and they have recently formed (as centuries of Yeoman Warders dead and gone spun in their graves) their own branch of the Civil Service Trade Union.

Below Tower Hill, the City's Speakers' Corner, TOWER BRIDGE [K5]—the last across the Thames before the sea—swings its improbable late Victorian Gothic over the river. Its low roadway can be raised to allow ships to go through, and this happens to the accompaniment of well-oiled clanking four or five times a day, as big a treat for children as the spot where the headsman's block once stood.

TRAFALGAR SQUARE [E4] WC2. Flanked by the massiveness of the National Gallery and National Portrait

Gallery, the pillared loftiness of St Martin-in-the-Fields, tall office buildings, Admiralty Arch and the shipping offices of Cockspur Street, Trafalgar Square is one of London's few planned public spaces, a sort of poor man's Place Vendome. The height of the Column (see NELSON'S COLUMN) pulls the Square together, and the fountains, particularly at night when they're floodlit, give it space and gaiety. A traditional venue for political rallies, the Square is always crowded on Christmas Eve, when carols are sung around the giant Norwegian Christmas tree, and on New Year's Eve, when the songs and doings are profaner. You can feed the pigeons, which are as much a part of the city as Nelson himself, have your photograph taken or just sit and rest your feet. Most people do all three.

TRAVEL AGENCIES. All over London, you will find reliable and efficient small agencies which will fix all details of your travel at no extra charge. They make their money by getting a commission from the shipping lines, railways, airlines and so on. Below are listed simply a few of the better known:

American Express Co., Inc., 6 Haymarket, SW1	WHI 4411
Ashton & Mitchell, 2 Old Bond St. W1	MAY 7222
Thos. Cook & Son Ltd., Berkeley St. W1	GRO 4000
Dean & Dawson Ltd., 81 Piccadilly, W1	GRO 3333
Frames Tours Ltd., 25 Denmark St. WC2	TEM 1522
Sir Henry Lunn Ltd., 172 New Bond St. W1	MAY 8444
Polytechnic Touring Association, 309 Regent St. W1	MAY 8100
Webster & Girling Ltd., 211 Baker St. NW1	WEL 6666

TROOPING THE COLOUR. One of London's most splendid pageants, the Colour is trooped by the Brigade of Guards in the presence of the Queen on Horse Guards Parade in early June each year. An unforgettable sight, you should get there early in the morning if you want to have a good place to see it from; tickets for the stands can sometimes be obtained from the London District Headquarters of the Horse Guards, Whitehall, SW1.

TUBES. The Tube, as London's underground railway is affectionately known, is one of the most efficient and convenient forms of public transport anywhere in the world. Stretching over sixty-seven miles of track, carrying six hundred and forty-one million passengers a year, the Tube has set standards in smoothness of operation, comfort and design, which are unequalled anywhere. Obviously the rush hour—8.30 to 9.30 in the morning, 5 to 6 at night—should be avoided if you want to be sure of a seat. You can go almost anywhere by Tube, and the Tube map is easy to understand. (See map page 134.)

TURKISH BATHS. In a world of rising prices, Turkish baths remain surprisingly reasonable. They remain, too, one of the best ways to get rid of a hangover. If you are an addict, you'll find your needs  well catered for at the premises listed below. If you've never had one before, try it just for the experience. You may find it terrible to be first boiled and then frozen, with a bit of pummelling thrown in, but the after-effect is worth it.

FOR MEN

Imperial Hotel, Russell Square, WC1   TER 4876
    Always open. Basic charge: 7/6
Savoy Turkish Baths, 92 Jermyn St. SW1   WHI 9552
    Always open. Basic charge: 8 a.m. to 8 p.m.—7/6
                                  8 p.m. to 8 a.m.—12/6

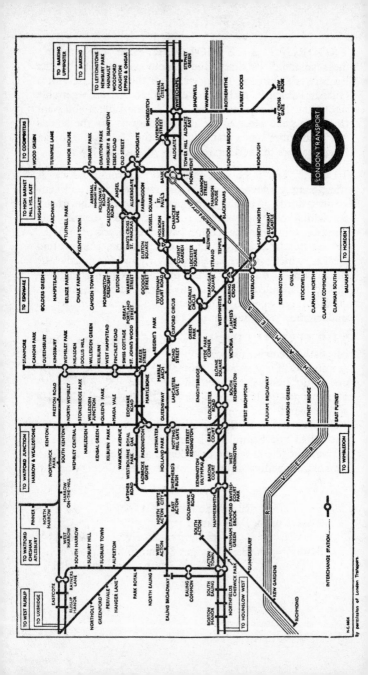

Dorchester Hotel, Park Lane, W1   MAY 8888
   9 a.m. to 6 p.m. Basic charge: 8/6.
Savoy Turkish Baths, 12 Duke of York St.   WHI 7125
SW1
   Monday to Friday: 9 a.m. to 8 p.m.
   Saturday: 9 a.m. to 4 p.m.
   Sunday: 10 a.m. to 4 p.m.
   Basic charge: 8/6

TUSSAUD'S, Madame [c2] Baker Street, NW1.
(WEL 3726. Tube to Baker Street.) You can still see the
founder in her dark dress and old poke bonnet, who brought
the original collection over from France shortly after the
French Revolution—appropriately immortalised among her
other wax-works. The exhibition is now run by her great-
great grandson. Most of the old models were destroyed by
fire in the twenties, but some still remain, many of them in
the Chamber of Horrors (down in the basement, 9d extra;
not for the squeamish or the very young). Madame Tussaud's is now an institution, and is visited every year by
hundreds of thousands of schoolchildren who goggle at
Henry VIII, stare with even greater awe at Len Hutton and
are uninterested in the effigies of politicians. Go there for
an hour on a wet afternoon. It's a London must. Open
10 a.m. to 6 p.m. (7 p.m. on Saturday and Sunday).
Admission 3/-. Children 1/-

U

UMBRELLA. There are two kinds of unbrella: those
that are used, and those that are carried. The former are
seen in great numbers in suburban trains and the City,
flapping and rusty and everyday looking; the latter parade
along Bond Street, Piccadilly, St James's and Pall Mall, as
slim and crisp and elegant as a Guards' officer on parade.
They are never under any circumstance opened They are the

twentieth century's equivalent of the sword, and very gallant they look, too, in the right hands. For where to get either kind, see SHOPPING.

UNDERGROUND. See TUBES.

V

VALETING. See CLEANERS.

VETERINARY SERVICES. If you've brought your pet with you to town and he's not standing up to the strain of city life, you need only telephone the Royal Society for the Prevention of Cruelty to Animals at 105 Jermyn Street, SW1 (WHI 7177 or 1651), and they will give you the name of a veterinary surgeon in your district. The Society also operates (from the same address) an emergency night service from 5 p.m. to 8 a.m. If you haven't enough cash to pay for a surgeon, the Society will give you the name of one of their free animal clinics.

VICE. London, they tell me, is a vicious city. The Sunday papers talk a lot about its depravity. And certainly, Piccadilly Circus and the dark streets that surround it are not without squalidness. But on the whole, London is remarkably free from organised vice, largely due to the stolid incorruptibility of an underpaid police force. If you want to find naughtiness, of course you'll find it. But you'll have to look quite hard. Don't believe everything you hear, and in particular, don't believe the spiv who hints at splendid goings-on in a little club he knows in Soho: you'll probably end up drinking filthy cocktails with a rabbit-faced blonde called Rosie, while six large men get larger and larger, and the room smaller.

W

WEATHER is as much a topic of conversation for Londoners as it is for everyone else in this weather-bound country. Suitable phrases like 'Raining again, I see', or 'Cold this morning', or 'Foggy last night', or 'Nippy, that east wind', or, more rarely, 'Nice morning', are standard conversational openings. However, Londoners like it. And no earthquakes have been recorded in the City's history. As the Duke of Wellington once said, 'For eight months, it is the best climate in the world. And the remaining four—damme, sir! I don't know a better.'

The radio and newspapers pay constant attention to it, and at the end of the television service every day is given a luxurious weather forecast, complete with maps covered in isobars. It you want detailed information beyond this about what's likely to happen in Paris the day after to-morrow, for example, telephone The Meteorologist—HOL 3434, extension 629, or go and look at the weather window in the Time-Life building at the Bond Street end of Bruton Street.

WELLINGTON MUSEUM. See APSLEY HOUSE.

WEMBLEY STADIUM. See EMPIRE STADIUM and POOL.

WESTMINSTER ABBEY [E6] (Tube to Westminster). No longer an Abbey (since the suppression of its monastery in 1560), it remains London's most royal and venerable church. No one knows how long a church has stood on the site, but we do know that Edward the Confessor is the first king to have been buried there, and that every English monarch has been crowned there since the Norman Conquest. Here rest the Coronation Chair and the Stone of Scone (see CORONATION CHAIR). Here too rests the Unknown Soldier, side by side with kings and statesmen, admirals and scientists, authors and actors, great men honoured by the nation. To walk through its grey quietness is to walk through nine hundred years of British history.

When you've had your fill of greatness, go out under the

cloisters and through the little gate into DEAN'S YARD, gentle and tree-shadowed, a quiet little backwater that the tide of panoply sweeps past without noticing.

WESTMINSTER CATHEDRAL [D6] Victoria, SW1 (Tube to Victoria, or 38 bus). The principal Roman Catholic cathedral of Britain, it was completed in 1903, and is in a Victorian–Byzantine style. Famous for its music, it's the seat of a cardinal.

WESTMINSTER HALL [E6] SW1 (Tube to Westminster). All that remains of the old Palace of Westminster, and now a part of the Houses of Parliament, it was here that English law was dispensed for many centuries, and beneath this oak roof that the dramatic trials of Charles I, Warren Hastings, Guy Fawkes and many others, unrolled. For details of when to see it, see HOUSES OF PARLIAMENT.

WHIPSNADE. See ZOOS.

WHITEHALL [E5] SW1. Curving grandly down from

Trafalgar Square to Westminster Bridge and the Houses of Parliament, Whitehall is made up almost entirely of Government offices: the War Office, the Admiralty, the Foreign Office, the Treasury and so on. On your left, New Scotland Yard; on your right, the Horse Guards Parade; in the centre of the street, the Cenotaph.

WIMBLEDON. (WIM 2244. Tube to Southfields or Wimbledon, thence bus.) The Wimbledon Lawn Tennis Championships remain the world's top tennis event. They are held at the end of June and beginning of July, and if you want to get in without

queueing, you should order a season ticket before 9th February by writing to: Wimbledon Tennis Championships, Church Road, SW19.

WREN CHURCHES. Of all Londoners, Sir Christopher Wren has left the loveliest memorial. Apart from St Paul's, his master work, the genius who rebuilt so much of the City after the Great Fire of 1666 left a score or more of churches which were, in their own way, just as fine. But many, alas, suffered from bombing in World War II. Some were completely destroyed, and nearly all of them damaged, some very badly. Among those destroyed completely, or so badly damaged as to be beyond reconstruction, were St Nicholas Cole Abbey, St Mary Aldermanbury, St Mildred's, Bread Street, St Lawrence Jewry, King Street, and St Alban's, Wood Street.

Some of the most famous, although badly damaged, are being restored. St Mary-le-Bow, Cheapside, for example, from whose two hundred and twenty-two foot high steeple Bow Bells—the Whittington Chimes—rang out to tell all Londoners within earshot that they were true Cockneys, is rising again, with the help of generous American gifts. So is St Clement Danes in the Strand, whose luckier 'Oranges and Lemons' bells survived, and which is to become a Royal Air Force chapel. The graceful steeple of St Bride's, Fleet Street (the tallest Wren built) soars up from an empty shell. Did you know that it was from this steeple that the basic design of wedding cakes—Bride cakes, they used to be called—was taken? And in St Bride's Parish Register is a note recording the baptism of one of London's lustiest sons: Samuel Pepys. Badly damaged, too, is the delightfully named St Andrew's by the Wardrobe in Queen Victoria Street, which was so called because it was just next door to the King's Great Wardrobe, and was used by the Masters of the King's State Apparel. Only the crypt of St Magnus the Martyr's, in Lower Thames Street, is open; and while St James's, Piccadilly, gutted during the War by fire, is being rebuilt, only the south aisle is open for services. In front of it is a memorial garden to Londoners who died in World War II.

Happily, a few of Wren's churches escaped with only slight damage, and one or two with none at all. Of these, you should not miss St Benet's in Queen Victoria Street, St Clement's in Clement's Lane (with its splendid carved pulpit), St Edmund the King and Martyr in Lombard Street, St Margaret Lothbury (with its Grinling Gibbons font), St Mary Aldermary in Queen Victoria Street (famous for its fan vaulting), or St Peter's, Cornhill, which many people claim as the earliest church of London.

WRESTLING. See BOXING and WRESTLING.

Z

ZEBRA CROSSINGS. Relative newcomers to London are the zebra crossings, whose black and white stripes mark the correct crossing places in busy streets. The theory is that once you've actually managed to establish one foot on one stripe, all the traffic stops and allows you to walk across unharmed. This, as I say, is the theory. Don't put too much faith in it, or you're liable to leave London with less feet than you started out with. But on the other hand, there's the nice feeling that if you do get knocked down on one of these, the motorist is going to have a rough time of it. And the best of luck to you.

ZOOS go one, two, three. First, *the* zoo in Regent's Park; second, Whipsnade on the Chiltern Hills; third, Chessington in Surrey.

The Regent's Park Zoo (PRI 3333), run by the Royal Zoological Society, covers thirty-five acres in the central north-west of London, and was first opened in 1828. It contains every kind of animal, bird, reptile, fish and insect you can think of, and lots that you can't. It opens at 9 a.m. in the summer (10 a.m. in winter) and closes at dusk or seven o'clock, whichever is earlier. Get the guide and information book from the offices at the Zoo to make sure you don't miss anything. It's a good 2/6 worth. Sunday mornings are for Fellows and their guests only (opening time for the public 2.30 p.m.). Feeding times (the animals, not the Fellows) are:

Chimpanzees' Tea Party—4.30 p.m. in summmer only, not Sundays, and weather permitting.

Eagles—3.30 p.m. except Wednesdays.

Lions and Tigers—3 p.m. in summer, 2 p.m. in winter.

Pelicans—2.30 p.m.

Penguins—12.30 and 4 p.m. in summer. 12.30 only in winter.

Sea Lions—12 noon and 3.30 p.m. in summer, 2.30 in winter.

Seals—4.30 p.m. in summer, 3.30 in winter.

Small Cats—11 a.m.

Wolves and Foxes—11.30 a.m.

To get there, take a 74 bus from Baker Street to the North Gate.

Whipsnade (DUNSTABLE 900, TOLL) is out in the country, five hundred acres of rolling greenness in the Chiltern Hills. Here you can really see the animals in their natural surroundings. It opens at 10 a.m. and closes at sunset or seven o'clock whichever is earlier (7.30 on Sundays). You can eat there perfectly well in an old farm house which has been converted, and buy the usual kind of fizzy lemonade at the usual kind of kiosks. If you're taking a large party for the day, get special terms by telephoning the Catering Manager, (DUNSTABLE 900, TOLL). Feeding times are (the animals, not you):

Kodiak Bears—3.35 p.m.

Leopards—4 p.m.

Lions—3.45 p.m.

Polar Bears—3.20 p.m.

Sea Lions—3 p.m.

Tigers—4.15 p.m.

(All times half-an-hour earlier during winter.)

During the summer, you can get a 726 Green Line coach from Baker Street straight to Whipsnade, which takes about an hour and a half. The rest of the year, you go by train from King's Cross to Dunstable, and thence by coach.

Finally, Chessington Zoo (EPSOM 413, TOLL), particularly amusing for children, but zoologically not up to the standard of the others. Its Pets' Corner and Circus and Playground and Punch and Judy Show more than make up for this, though. You can eat there perfectly well, too. Go by 714 Green Line Coach from Hyde Park Corner, or by train from Waterloo to Chessington South. It takes about an hour to get there.